The Moral Bond of Community

The Moral Bond of Community
Justice and Discourse in
Christian Morality

BERNARD V. BRADY

GEORGETOWN UNIVERSITY PRESS / WASHINGTON, D.C.

Georgetown University Press, Washington, D.C.
© 1998 by Georgetown University Press. All rights reserved.
Printed in the United States of America

10   9   8   7   6   5   4   3   2   1   1998

Library of Congress Cataloging-in-Publication Data

Brady, Bernard Vincent, 1957–
    The moral bond of community : justice and discourse in Christian
morality / Bernard Brady.
        p.   cm.
    "Chapter 2 . . . originally appeared in Journal for Peace and
Justice Studies, v. 7, no. 2."—CIP galley.
    Includes bibliographical references and index.
    1. Christian ethics. 2. Storytelling—Religious aspects—
Christianity. 3. Christianity and justice. 4. Christian ethics—
Catholic authors.   I. Title.
BJ1241.B77   1998
241—dc21
    ISBN 0-87840-690-5 (cloth).
    ISBN 0-87840-691-3 (pbk.)   98-5663

For my mother's mother, Katie Leneghan
God love you in your one hundred second year of life
and for my father's brother, Leo Patrick (Fr. Ned) Brady, C.P.,
as a child I remember you discussing justice with my father,
you unknowingly planted some seeds

Contents

Preface

I hope the following scenario never happens.

There is a crisis in America. We are on the verge of war. The next few days are crucial. Will we bomb that foreign country to stop their aggression? Some of us will trust and support the decision of our elected officials, whatever their decision. Others of us will have family members and friends in the military. Perhaps they are already on the scene, waiting for the command. We do not want our loved ones harmed and thus would not want war. If, however, there is war, we will not speak out against it for fear of weakening our government's resolve. There will also be a group of us adamantly opposed to the war. There will be those among us who are sure that war is the right thing to do. The largest group of us might be those who are not yet sure where we stand.

If the above scenario were to happen, there would be an all-out attempt by people of both opinions to convince everyone else that their position is morally correct. This will be done in a number of ways: We will witness a variety of people "telling their stories." We will hear, first hand, what it is like to suffer under a repressive government. Others will tell us of the horrors of being in a war. We will also hear stories of past American wars, memories of futility in Vietnam and "smart bombs" in Iraq. Those who tell such stories want their listeners to be moved by the stories.

On the verge of war, we will hear protesters challenging the war effort (and perhaps broader issues of U.S. involvement in global affairs). These people, with passionate words and strong condemnation, will indict the United States for its planned killing spree. On the other side, if the United States decided not to go to war, there are those who would charge Americans with moral irresponsibility for ignoring the victims of aggression.

If there were this crisis in the land, there would also be examples of less impassioned moral discourse. Television stations, newspapers, and campuses would sponsor reasoned debates illustrating both sides of the issue. In workplaces and families, people would consider reasons for or against going to war. Defenders of both positions would appeal to your intellect and explain why going to war is just or unjust.

In the end, however, the decision to go to war is a decision outside of our control. The decision will be made by politicians whose primary responsibility is to promote the common good of this country in relation to the global community. It is they who will make the moral choice about war and about the tactics in war. Their decisions will put American lives at risk. Their decisions will determine the amount of death and destruction the world will witness. Thus they must realize the moral implications of such a decision.

This scenario illustrates a fact that is not commonly recognized; namely, that when we talk about morality, when we think about morality, we promote our moral ideas in a variety of ways. James Gustafson has described the varieties of moral discourse to include narrative, prophetic, ethical, and policy.[1] He suggests these as ideal types. They are stereotypical ways people approach morality. Narrative discourse refers to the use of story as a form of communicating moral wisdom and virtues. Jesus, for example, in his use of parables, illustrates the significance of stories in moral communication. Prophetic discourse begins with a denouncement of a particular policy or social practice. The prophet uses strong, passionate language to charge society with a moral crime. The Hebrew Scriptures witness a number of prophets whose message as well as style of moral communication informs us today.

Ethical discourse is the "process of giving reasons for action."[2] Ethics presents reasonable arguments (grounded and marked by consistency and coherency), highlights morally relevant distinctions, and offers precise definitions of moral terms. Many considerations of morality in college classrooms are ethical discourse. Introductory textbooks in morality, for example, begin by discussing the types of ethical theories. Moral discourse is not limited to narrative, prophetic, and ethical. Morally serious people make decisions and engage in policy discourse every day. Persons make life and lifestyle choices; families make decisions about how to spend time and money; institutions make choices about hiring and workplace relations; governments make choices about supporting citizens, going to war, etc. In contrast to the prophet or even the ethicist, "The policy maker has to know what is possible, as well as what is the right thing to do."[3] The policy maker often has to decide between moral purism and compromise. As Gustafson notes, "What is desirable is always related to what is possible."[4] Policy decisions, whether intended or not, are often moral decisions as they affect the lives of individual persons and relationships between people.

It is Gustafson's judgment, and I think he is correct, that Christian moral discourse ought to include all four forms of moral discourse. Some people are called to be prophetic; some by inclination and circumstance are responsible for policy. Some people are suspicious of emotionally packed language and are more convinced by appeals to reason. Others tend to use narratives to communicate a moral point or a moral point of view. While each of these four forms is necessary, none alone is sufficient to capture the whole of Christian moral life. This is especially borne out in a discussion of justice. Certainly many philosophers and theologians have offered theories of justice. Such exercises in ethical discourse present conceptual interpretations of the term. Prophets often have little time for abstract theory. The prophet's words, however, many provide the enthusiasm and energy through which one might engage in more abstract thinking. Prophets and indeed ethicists may have little in common with the administrator, manager, or politician whose role it is to bring justice to concrete circumstances.

This book is about moral discourse and justice. The first, and more general task, is to present an understanding of the four different forms of moral discourse. Recognition of these forms invites broader and fuller conversations about morality. It also invites the reader to see how he or she fits into such a scheme and how he or she might use a different form of moral discourse when appropriate. The discerning person knows that sometimes a simple witness to justice is more appropriate than a lecture on justice. This first task, however, is in service of another purpose. The book aims to develop a conceptualization of justice informed by the Bible and human experience in relationships.

The book weaves these two purposes. The first chapter analyzes the narrative form of moral discourse and then examines two biblical narratives, the story of persons being created in the image of God and the Exodus event. The chapter illustrates the primary place of narrative in moral discourse and provides foundational themes for the consideration justice. The biblical citations throughout the book are from the *New Oxford Annotated Bible: New Revised Standard Version* (New York: Oxford University Press, 1991). The second chapter examines the writings and message on justice of the eighth century prophets in the Hebrew Bible. The chapter includes a discussion of a legacy of the prophets, the prophetic form of moral discourse. This section originally appeared in

Journal for Peace and Justice Studies, vol. 7, no. 2. The third chapter draws some conclusions on justice from the Hebrew Scriptures and relates those to the life and teaching of Jesus. Particular attention is given to Jesus' teaching on the Kingdom of God. The fourth chapter describes ethical discourse and ethical theory in light of the biblical material. Building on the earlier chapters, the fifth chapter offers a conceptualization of justice through a reflection on different types of relationships. The final chapter addresses the fourth form of moral discourse, policy, and considers the questions of the relation of morality to law and justice to policy. The title is adapted from the title of Arthur Dyck's book, *Rethinking Rights and Responsibilities: The Moral Bonds of Community* (Cleveland: The Pilgrim Press, 1994).

As I complete this book, I am grateful to be part of a supportive learning community at the University of St. Thomas. A semester sabbatical and additional lightening of my teaching responsibilities granted by the university, as well as financial support from the Aquinas Foundation, allowed me to pursue this project. For that I am very thankful. Thanks also to my colleagues who read parts of the book and offered their support and expert commentary. I could not have imagined working with a more helpful and professional staff than I experienced with Georgetown University Press.

It is a rare occasion when one gets to publicly acknowledge one's debt to one's family. Parents are supposed to be moral teachers for their children, but I must say that my kids have been moral teachers for me. I am blessed with four teachers, Mark, Patrick, Ned, and Ellen. Each one has a unique personality and each one's set of dispositions and attitudes informs my moral character. Their love directs my life. My deepest gratitude, however, goes to my wife Cindy. Her life and her work continually witness the possibilities of love and justice.

Gratitude is not so much a resting point as it is a directive for action. The following words from Gustafson capture my sentiment:

> Out of a sense of gratitude should come a concern for justice. Having received, a people should not take more than is their due; they should not deprive others of life's resources for the sake of their own luxurious pleasure and conveniences. It is out of a sense of gratitude that both moral volition and an imperative arise. God has freely given life to us; we, in thankfulness to him, are to be concerned for others' well-being as he has been concerned for ours.[5]

CHAPTER ONE

You Don't Have Anything
If You Don't Have Stories

I will tell you something about stories, they aren't just
entertainment. Don't be fooled. . . . You don't have anything
if you don't have stories.

—Leslie Marmon Siko

NARRATIVE: THE BEGINNING OF MORAL DISCOURSE

Stories or narratives serve many functions in our lives. They help us
to relax and to forget our daily worries, our burdens and our anxieties.
They divert our attention, amuse us, and invite us to experience new
and different ideas and feelings (or numb us so we have no feelings at
all!). We turn to narratives every day, whether we watch TV or a
movie, read a book, or even talk to a friend. However, as the above
quote suggests, there is something more to narratives than just that
they might be pleasing to us or that they help us pass the time. It is
through narratives that we are able to understand our lives and interpret
our experience. Narratives form and inform our values, our dispositions
and how we "see" the world. As the quotation proposes, narratives are
central to our self-identity. "Narrative" includes not only stories but
parables, rituals, artwork, and even the lives of persons. This first
chapter has four sections. The first will consider the moral significance
of narratives and discuss the different types of narratives. It will suggest
the importance of narratives as the principal form of moral discourse.
The following sections will consider the biblical narratives as the primary
source for Christian moral reflection. The second section will address
methodological issues (or "how to" issues) of interpreting biblical narratives. The third section will examine the first Creation story in Genesis
and consider its implications for understanding what it means to be a
person. The final section will look at the story of the Exodus and the

portrait of God presented in that story. Both narratives will direct our understanding of justice. Let's begin then with a discussion of narrative discourse.

The Power of a Good Story

There is a secret about moral discourse good preachers know that some professors of ethics are unaware of. That secret is that a good story has more impact on people than a tightly argued ethical theory. Indeed, some would argue that narrative is *the* medium of moral communication.[1] A good story informs our moral imagination, our moral vision, and our moral character in ways logical generalizations, clear arguments, and rules do not. Richard Gula is not exaggerating when he states, "We live more by stories than we do by rules."[2] Jesus seemed to appreciate this, given that he often used parables when he taught. To begin consideration of the moral significance of narrative, let us look at a narrative. The following is a story I have come across in a number of places. It serves well to introduce us to narrative form.

"If Not Higher"

Once, in a small village in Eastern Europe, there lived a very respected and well-loved rabbi. Every Friday morning the rabbi left his home to take a walk in the woods. When he returned several hours later, he was tired and worn, yet his presence radiated a deep peace and love. After a time and much discussion, the members of the rabbi's community took to the idea that while gone on those Friday mornings, the rabbi "ascended to heaven and sat in the presence of God." Gradually the word spread about this holy man, this man who ascends to God, and his reputation grew throughout the region.

A young rabbinical student from a neighboring village heard this story of the rabbi but could not bring himself to believe it. So he traveled to the village to find out for himself whether the story was true. Early one Friday morning, the young man hid near the rabbi's house. He watched as the rabbi awoke, said his prayers, ate a small breakfast, and dressed himself in peasant's clothes. As the rabbi left his home, he picked up his ax and went into the woods. From a distance the young man followed the rabbi. The rabbi made his way through the woods and gathered sticks and logs into a large bundle of wood. He carried the wood to a small house on the edge of the forest where an elderly widow and her invalid son lived. The rabbi worked through the morning gathering, chopping, and stacking the wood alongside the woman's house. When enough wood for the week was stacked, the rabbi walked home through the woods.

The young man stayed in the village and became a student of the rabbi. When he heard, as he often did, the villagers boasting of their rabbi who "ascends to heaven," he would quietly respond, "if not higher."

"If Not Higher" has the usual features of a story. There is a unity, that is, it has a beginning, a middle, and an end. Though short, this story has other features that make it compelling. Specifically, "If Not Higher" has characters with some appeal or intrigue to the reader, namely, a curious or mysterious holy man, a group of admirers or followers of this man, and a rather cynical young man. (Vicious or gross characters might also capture the reader's imagination.) If you were asked, "What is this story about?" you might be hard pressed to limit your comments to one point. The story, again though very short, is about several things.

Gustafson suggests that "narratives shape the ethos of a . . . community, and by participating in the community, they shape and direct vision and character" of community members.[3] In "If Not Higher" the community coalesces around their rabbi and the story of their rabbi. The tale gives the community pride, and it serves to ground their relationship to one another. By telling and retelling this story, they are also saying, "We are the people of this rabbi." Ironically, and perhaps even humorously, the admiring followers miss the very point of the rabbi's life! But the story, nonetheless, that the rabbi "ascends to heaven and sits in the presence of God," gives the community an identity as well as inspiration. However, "If Not Higher" is not primarily about the community. Like most compelling narratives, "If Not Higher" has stories within the story.

The most obvious "moral" to "If Not Higher" is that service to those in need is the highest calling of a person. Such service is correlated to being with God. The rabbi's "real life" tells this message. The story is then about holiness, but again, it is about more than this. The main character of "If Not Higher" is not the rabbi. Nothing really happens to him; he is the occasion for the story. "If Not Higher" is about the young man. The story affirms his curiosity and questioning. In comparison, the people who blindly believe the story seem foolish. The young man's quest, his revelation, and his conversion from doubt to discipleship, are as much the message of the story as is the "spirituality" of the rabbi. The rabbi's life journey to serve God and the young man's journey to learn how to serve God converge in this story.

"If Not Higher" illustrates at least two characteristics of narrative as moral discourse. The first is the "magnetic appeal" of narratives and the second is that narratives answer the foundational questions of moral life in a particular manner. Concerning the magnetic appeal: What makes this story a good story, indeed a classic narrative, is that it offers the possibility for the reader or listener to be drawn into the story and to participate in the story. The reader, like the cynical young man, is given an opportunity to be curious and restless. The story invites the reader to share the insight, the revelation and transformation of the young man. If there is an effect on the reader, if indeed the reader is in some sense caught up in the story, then something interesting has occurred. This is especially true if the reader, while relating to the story as a whole, cannot relate to the particulars of the story. Perhaps the reader is not Jewish; maybe the reader has never met a rabbi nor been to Eastern Europe. Perhaps the reader has never held an ax, chopped wood or visited an elderly woman and her invalid son! If this is true, that the reader can relate to the story in general but cannot relate to the particulars of the story, then something worthy of note has happened. This story has suggested some common experience or communicated some truth or reality to the reader even though the context of the storyteller and the reader are practically "worlds apart." How can this be? How can stories from other cultures, from other time periods, or from other religious traditions be formative and informative to us? Good narratives or, perhaps better stated, classic narratives, transcend contextual particularities. Like a magnet, they draw the reader or hearer into the questions at hand, whether such questions be the highest or most base of human existence. Such narratives have the strength to bridge cultures and provide persons with a place to meet.

The second characteristic of narrative as a form of moral discourse is that narratives prioritize the moral question of "being" over the moral question of "doing." The two fundamental questions of the moral life are: "Who am I to be?" and "What am I to do?" or posed communally, "Who are we to be?" and "What are we to do?" These two questions, of course, are not mutually exclusive; they are, rather, mutually informative. The first question focuses on the interiority, or the being, of the person. It addresses personal qualities and characteristics, what James Gustafson refers to as the "sort of person one is." Think for a moment of a person you think to be morally good. Once you get a specific person in mind, think of three or four words you would use to describe this person. Is your morally good person, honest, trusting, loving, always willing to help others? Perhaps other virtues come to mind when you think of her. How do you know this person is good? You know the person is good because you have seen her be good. You have witnessed the person, time and time again, live out these characteristics. Actions are performed by people; they are expressions of personal characteristics. Her actions, her doing, in a sense, illustrate the person she is. If your morally good person acted contrary to the virtue or virtues you associate with her, you would be shocked. What is important to note here is that the person is good not merely because she does the right thing. She is good because she has the interior qualities or characteristics that enable her to do the right thing. The logic between being and doing is circular. If one's actions reflect one's character, then it must also be said that one's actions, especially if repeated over time, influence one's character.

The power of narrative is that it calls on the subjectivity of the person. As the person is engaged in the story, she becomes engaged in herself. Good narratives, like "If Not Higher" have stories within stories. While narratives can address both the being and doing questions, they primarily force the question of being. They illustrate virtues and encourage certain character traits, but do not tell the reader exactly what to do in specific situations. Good narratives, while not denying the importance of right and wrong actions, tend to focus on the morals of being rather than the morals of doing as the primary question of moral reflection. The narrative approach to moral discourse might be likened to a tennis match. The storyteller serves a plot or a hero to the reader, and the burden of response is on the reader. Gustafson writes, "Narratives . . . do not provide single, clear, and argued answers." Rather, they serve to illuminate "what is at stake and what conduct might be most appropriate."[4]

If there is one group of people who know the power of a good narrative, it is advertisers. The commercials that catch our eye are often similar in form to "If Not Higher." There is a unity, compelling characters, and a message somewhat related to the two fundamental questions of the moral life. Obviously, commercials aim to inform our action. We ought to buy the product! However, they also often make claims, seemingly moral claims, concerning the first question: Who am I to be? Through drama, humor, song, and many other means, advertisers tell us that this product will make us feel better about ourselves. This product will make us more attractive, sexier, smarter, or more sophisticated. Indeed some advertising suggests that we would be lesser human beings without this product.

Art and Ritual as Narrative

Understanding the performing arts as narrative is an obvious next step. Dance, plays, movies, and operas, after all, tell stories. However, considering the visual arts as narrative might not seem so obvious. But sculpture, painting, even architecture can be understood as narratives. They can tell a story, reveal a text of an historical period, evoke thoughts and feelings from an audience. Indeed, like the reader of a story, the viewer of a work of art might be compelled to address the moral questions of being and doing described above.

The university where I teach offers an interesting illustration of this. The university has two campuses, each boasting a large, eye-catching bronze sculpture in the commons area. The sculptures, however, tell very different stories and indeed evoke very different moral dispositions. In a prominent place on one campus sits "The Entrepreneur." "The Entrepreneur" is a striking bronze statue of a blindfolded man chiseling himself out of a large, rough rock. It depicts the "self-made man." The man's head, arms, torso, and thighs have already been fashioned from the stone. His right hand holds a hammer poised high above his head, ready to strike a chisel grasped tightly in his left hand. The sculpture captures him forming his right knee. "The Entrepreneur" is creating himself out of a natural state of inanimate material. His job is nearly complete. Soon he will emerge, freed from his existence in stone. "The Entrepreneur" is a narrative. It, in a sense, tells a story. The piece communicates a strong message about being a person. Without words, it says that we can and do "make ourselves." It highlights individuality, separateness, and self-determination as the essential elements of being human. The observer of the statue becomes a participant in the narrative when he or she allows this narrative to intersect with his or her life. "The Entrepreneur" evokes certain questions of character in the participant. Am I a self-made person? Am I self-directing? Am I as autonomous as I should be?

In an equally prominent place on the other campus sits "Constellation Earth." The narrative of this work is strikingly different, indeed opposite of "The Entrepreneur." While the latter highlights autonomy and self-determination, the former suggests community, interdependence, and cooperation. "Constellation Earth" is a globe, or rather a statue of seven people forming a globe. The people, whose genders are quite evident (they are naked) but whose races or nationalities are not, are positioned where the seven continents are found on earth. The people are stretched and turned so that they are holding on to one another as they extend to form the sphere. The communion of figures in "Constellation Earth" is striking when compared to the individual in "The Entrepreneur." "Constellation Earth" evokes questions of contribution to the whole, partnership with others, and the necessary feature of being persons, namely reaching out toward others. Both works of art tell a story. Both provide the possibility of observers becoming participants and being informed or supported or challenged in their understanding of what it means to be a person.

Along with stories and art, we are surrounded by other types of narratives. Think, for example, of rituals, religious or otherwise, that you have participated in. Underlying the actions and words is a "subtext" that expresses certain values, whether the participants are consciously aware of them or not. In Christian Churches, the very dramatic yet subtle rituals of communion and baptism tell stories and indicate appropriate moral attitudes and dispositions. Organizations and groups, indeed families, have rituals that function, as was suggested above, to shape the ethos of the group and form the vision and character of its members.

Persons' Lives as Narrative

The most powerful narratives for persons often are the narratives of the lives of other people. Normally, the lives of one's parents are most influential in the moral dispositions of a person. While parents give children rules and expectations (and perhaps back up those rules with punishments and rewards) that form character, the lasting imprint on our morals has to be our interpretations of our parents' lives. The stories of how our parents treated us, how we witnessed them treating each other, and how we saw them relate to other people serve as a ground for our moral imagination. At a young age, we probably mimicked their words and actions. As we mature, their influence might be seen at a deeper level. Namely, their lasting effect would be the formation of the basic beliefs, attitudes, and dispositions we have. It is at this level that narratives have their lasting influence. Narratives form our moral senses and feelings before they form our moral intellect. This is not a deterministic view. We can and do choose between narratives. Indeed the process of moral maturity demands that we make choices between competing narratives. The narratives of our family, for example, can conflict with the narratives of popular culture. In the lives of my students, I see young men and women who define themselves against the narratives of their parents and those who affirm the narratives of their parents. The Christian tradition is full of martyrs, saints, teachers, and leaders whose lives have influenced the lives of others.

So far, the discussion of narratives has focused on things external to the reader. One hears a story, looks at a work of art, and witnesses the lives of others. These forms of narrative all stand outside the person. Yet we can speak of narrative in another way. In a very real sense, our lives and the lives of all persons can be described through narrative and as a narrative. Each of us has a story, a history marked by events, persons, loves, hardships, and choices that helped form who we are today. Like the young man in "If Not Higher," the narrative of our life has intersected with the narratives of the lives of many others and has offered us new visions of horizons and of day-to-day attitudes. As William Spohn writes, a person's "identity and character are like an unfolding story or a script that is still being written."[5] A person can get a sense of the narrative aspect of his life by recalling the process of becoming friends with another. When a level of trust and respect is attained, new friends usually tell each other stories about their lives. These stories give the other insight into the character of the other.

May the Best Narrative Win?

The lingering problem with narratives is that there are so many of them! Recall the two statues at the university where I teach. Which one, "The Entrepreneur" or "Constellation Earth," gives a truer picture of what it means to be a person? Which one better illustrates the essential characteristics of human life? How does one decide? Moreover, if a judgment is made concerning the adequacy of such a judgment, how does one share that judgment or speak of that judgment with other people? Herein lie the weaknesses associated with narrative as a form of moral discourse.

I have talked to a number of people to get their thoughts concerning "The Entrepreneur" and "Constellation Earth." Since the statues rest on different campuses, miles from each other, and they narrate such diverse messages, it is difficult from the works themselves to say they complement each other. People are compelled to prefer one over the other. Which statue appeals to you the most? Is it "The Entrepreneur" with its promotion of self-determination and autonomy or is it "Constellation Earth" with its promotion of unity and reaching out towards others? Maybe this is an unfair question given that you have never seen the pieces, but if you were to prefer one over the other, could you explain that preference to another person? What is it about the piece that draws you to it? Your answer might be that you can relate to it better. "The Entrepreneur" or "Constellation Earth" is affirmed by your experience or by your hopes and vision, in other words, by elements of your personal narrative. Let us say that you choose "Constellation Earth" and I choose "The Entrepreneur." How could we talk? How would we try to have each other see our view? You might say to me that "The Entrepreneur" presents a distortion of morality and the nature of the human person. Who, for example, told the character in the statue how to fashion himself? Did someone give him the hammer and chisel? Is he able to do, indeed to learn, all those things necessary for social life by himself? Can you really form yourself in isolation? On the other hand, I may say that I get myself out of bed in the morning. I go to work and take responsibility for my job and my life. I earned my degree. I have made choices that have made me who I am. If I did not take responsibility for my life, I would be like that lifeless rock "The Entrepreneur" carved himself out of.

What we have here is people, you and I, from differing narratives, trying to make sense of our world views for another. Some stories, perhaps "If Not Higher," seem able to transcend such particularities. Other narratives seem too parochial and contextually bound. Attempts to explain or convince others of the truthfulness of our narratives usually follow two general patterns. One we might call "circular logic"; the other we might call "search for common ground." Through the circular logic argument, one attempts to justify one's position by referring to other aspects of one's own narrative or tradition. Sometimes people who defend religious traditions work in this kind of language. For example, if you ask them, "How do you know God exists?" They might answer, "Because the Bible told me so." This type of defense of a position is "sectarian." Michael Perry writes that a sectarian argument "relies on experiences or premises that have little if any authority beyond the confines of one's own moral or religious community."[6] The circular or sectarian argument, while authoritative to one person, is not persuasive to the nonbeliever. One might say this is more preaching than dialogue.

When one moves outside one's community, tradition, or narrative, one must rely on a different form of moral discourse. If one is to speak to communities other than one's own community, one must, as suggested by Perry, try to "elaborate one's position in a manner intelligible to those who speak a different religious or moral language—to the point to translating one's position, to the extent possible, into a shared ('mediating') language."[7]

The lingering problem, as stated above, with narratives is there are so many of them. Even within communities or families, people are informed by a variety of narratives. Think for example of the many narratives playing in your life. Take your position on sex and sexuality for example. If you reflect seriously on your moral views here, you could probably list a variety of narratives that you have accepted or rejected in the formation of your conscience. How do you choose between the narrative of culture versus the narrative from Christianity? Is there a guiding idea or principle that helps you decide among competing claims? Not all the narratives can be true.

Let me give another example to illustrate the problem of narratives. A few years back, I watched a documentary on television about the Ku Klux Klan. The documentary cameras took the audience to a KKK summer family picnic. While much of the conversation was repulsive, what particularly stuck out in my mind was a game the children played. It was called, "Kill the Nigger." One unfortunate child was designated to be the "nigger" and then was chased around the park by the other children. The narrative of white supremacy and hatred of others was a ritual part of the upbringing of those kids. How can a fifteen-year-old son of a KKK member have any tolerance, much less respect, for another fifteen-year-old boy in his class who is not white? Narratives can encourage and sustain hate and injustice as much as they can evoke love and service. But who is to say that the KKK has it wrong and that I have it right? Once I try to reach out to you and explain why I think the KKK is based on a lie, why I find their beliefs morally repulsive, and I begin to give you reasons, I move from narrative discourse to ethical discourse.

Narratives themselves rarely help us to adjudicate between competing claims. We must appeal to some source or standard outside the narratives but related to the narratives. We must search for some common ground, some rational basis on which to make appeal.

"Truth" is an interesting topic when considering narrative discourse. A story may not be true, but it may illustrate some truth.

Professional storyteller Rose Schaper, for example, begins many of her stories with the phrase, "There once was a time and there once wasn't." The events in the story "If Not Higher" probably never happened. It is fiction. Like a figure of speech, it may not be true in a literal or historical sense, but it may express truth on a different level. I remember one time I was playing with my two-year-old daughter and my five-year-old son and it was getting near dinner time. Seeking consensus on the fact that it was about time to eat, I announced, "I am so hungry I could eat a horse!" My daughter laughed and said, "Dad, you can't eat a horse." My son, realizing that I was exaggerating but indeed was hungry, laughed at his sister's response. She did not get the joke. I was not lying when I said, "I am so hungry I could eat a horse!" I was not intentionally trying to deceive my kids. But my daughter, taking this literally, could not understand the truth I was trying to convey. So a story may not be true ("If Not Higher"), but it may express some truth. Likewise, a story might be true (there really was a KKK picnic), but it may express or be based on a lie. To discern truthfulness on the first level is a very different procedure than for discerning truthfulness on the second level.

Narratives are an essential component of moral discourse. Narratives initiate thinking about morality. As this section has indicated, there is, however, more to moral communication than stories. We will build on this theme in the following chapters of the book. This introduction to narrative discourse will help us understand the role biblical narratives ought to play in the life of the Christian community. The stories addressed in the following sections of this chapter are to Christians as the story of the rabbi was to his community. The story of persons being created in the image of God, the topic of section three, and the story of God liberating the people from slavery, the topic of section four, ought to shape the character of individual Christians and indeed the Christian community. We are the people of this God. These stories are foundations on which to build a moral perspective. Before we look at these stories, however, a few words need to be said about biblical interpretation. This is the topic of the following section.

THE BIBLE AND CONTEMPORARY MORALITY

The Bible contains the principle narratives for Christian life. These narratives give the Christian community and the individual Christian a sense of identity, value, and direction. Christians are "people of this book." The Bible forms and informs community and persons and, as such, it holds a primary place in Christian moral reflection. The narratives mediate, but do not fully resolve the problems of competing narratives. Christians have always taken seriously the invocation to use the Scripture to teach, correct, and train people. This point is not controversial. There is, however, a great deal of controversy on how the Bible ought to be interpreted. There are many ways Christians use the Bible as a source of moral guidance and wisdom. We hear the Bible read and preached every Sunday in worship and liturgy. Christians privately pray over and meditate on biblical passages and stories. My concern in this section is not to comment on liturgical or private use of the Bible (although my comments would relate to preaching on biblical texts). My concern here is with the appropriate use of the Bible in articulating and defending a public Christian moral vision. If one is making a public or a formal moral presentation or argument, that is, if one is using the Bible to try to convince other Christians about a particular moral concern, he or she must use the Bible in a way that is intelligible, logical, and truthful. Before we examine particular texts, it is important to make some initial comments on using the Bible in moral reflection.

Two Poles of Interpretation

There are two characteristic poles or extremes in biblical interpretation. The first is "fundamentalism" and the second is referred to as "proof-texting." Neither of these methods is supported in this book because they both, in very different ways, ignore or downplay the complexity of relating an ancient text from an ancient civilization to life as we know and experience it. Let's describe these two positions and then discuss the possibilities for a middle way between them.

There are two beliefs of fundamentalism relevant to the present task. First, fundamentalism holds that the Bible is the sole source of moral wisdom. The Bible is thus always "immediately relevant to a contemporary issue."[8] No interpretative tools or other sources of moral knowledge are needed. Fundamentalism justifies this view because of a second belief, namely that God is the sole author of the Bible. If God is the sole author of the Bible, then the environment and indeed predispositions of the human author have little or no significance for understanding the text. As Scripture scholars Raymond Brown and Sandra Schneiders write, "The author's limited world view becomes irrelevant in interpreting the text."[9] Fundamentalism sees the humans involved in writing the Bible more as note-takers transcribing the words inspired by God than as authors or editors. Fundamentalism then ignores crucial differences (linguistic, geographical, cultural, socioeconomic, philosophical, political, even religious) between the world in which the text was written and our world.[10]

The second extreme method of using the Scripture in moral conversation is "proof-texting." If fundamentalism is fully dependent on the Bible, this second method is fully independent of the Bible. Proof-texting consults the Bible in order to "prove" an opinion formed using nonbiblical sources. In other words, you first figure out your opinion of something, perhaps based on economic theory or military theory or criminal justice theory or political theory or some moral theory, and then look for biblical texts to "prove" your opinion. All you need is a single quotation. "Proof-texting" does not take seriously the idea that the Bible ought to inform the Christian life. It does not allow biblical themes, persons, ideas, and narratives to directly affect opinions and conclusions. It is not wrong to consult and be informed by nonbiblical sources. Indeed good moral arguments demand such information. The challenge to those who proof-text the Bible is whether or not they take the biblical material seriously and in all its complexity.

The Complex Middle Way

While a full theory of biblical interpretation appropriate for every book and passage in the Bible is beyond the scope of this book (and far beyond the competence of this writer!), a bit needs to be said about biblical interpretation. To be brief, but clear, the responsibilities of appropriate biblical interpretation will be described in five points.

First, the interpreter must identify the criteria used for choosing one text over another. In other words, the interpreter must give some account of why certain texts were chosen. This present book, for example, seeks to examine biblical material related to the topic of justice. It is not about the whole of biblical morality, though it examines texts from a variety of biblical sources. This book will examine several texts that have been historically significant in the Christian tradition. The determinative criteria then are the place of these texts in the Christian tradition as well as their relevance to the topic of justice.

Second, the text ought to be recognized as a particular literary style. There are a variety of types of literature in the Bible. James

Gustafson notes, "Scripture witnesses a great variety of moral values, moral norms, and principles through many different kinds of biblical literature: moral law, visions of the future, historical events, moral precepts, paraenetic instruction, parables, dialogues, wisdom sayings, allegories. They are not in a simple way reducible to a single theme."[11] A parable is different from a law which is different from a proverb. This difference demands differing interpretation. In this chapter, as well as the two following chapters, we will address some specifics of several of these types, namely mythic narrative, prophetic language, and parables.

Third, the text ought to be understood within the wider context of its place within the book from which it comes and indeed within the Bible as a whole. On many occasions, in and out of the classroom, I have heard people cite Exodus 20:13, "Do not kill" as the sum of the biblical morality on respect for human life. This is a crucial text for Christian ethics; however, it is not the only text. Chapter 21 in Exodus, for example, speaks of the possible justification for capital punishment. Thus, "Do not kill" ought not to be understood as an absolute moral principle in the Hebrew Scripture. The point here is that an honest use of the Bible takes into account the context of the story or passage. A Christian cannot simply quote a biblical passage without giving a context and expect other Christians to be convinced of his moral conclusions.

Fourth, there must be an attempt to understand what the text meant to the original community. This is the "exegetical" task. The purpose of this task is to get a sense of what the text meant to the original community. William Spohn states, "The meaning of a specific scriptural passage *then* has a controlling influence on its meaning *now*."[12] Quite often, however, this meaning is not evident to the contemporary reader. Those who want to use Scripture, then, in moral arguments must rely on the work of biblical scholars and serious students of the Bible to help them with this task. In the words of Richard Hays, "Serious exegesis is a basic requirement. Texts used in ethical arguments should be understood as fully as possible in their historical and literary context."[13]

The fifth responsibility of the person using the Bible in a public moral argument is the "hermeneutical" task. This interpretive process is a circular activity. It involves a genuine dialogue, a going back and forth between two realms, our particular historical experience and the original meaning of biblical text. This responsibility needs to be considered in greater detail.

On Appropriate Interpretation

There are four points here. The first two, as well as the fourth, distinguish the hermeneutical process from fundamentalism and the third distinguishes it from proof-texting.

First, a responsible approach to interpretation recognizes a dual authorship of the Bible. In the words of Brown and Schneiders, "the Bible has divine as well as human authorship."[14] This makes interpretation more complex for it suggests that the time and place in which the text was written have a determinative effect on the meaning of the text. The Bible is the word of God, or better stated, the Bible is God's self-communication in human words. The hermeneutical task struggles with the "complexity of the capacity of biblical language to bring expression of God's 'mind,' 'will,' and 'person.'"[15] Language, biblical or otherwise is, after all, a human construct reflecting the human condition. Again, quoting Brown and Schneiders, "God as the author of Scripture may be understood in terms of the *authority* who gives rise to the biblical books rather than in the sense of *writing* author."[16]

Second, the context makes a difference and interpreters must make some sense of these differences. The particularities of the time when the Bible was written affect what the Bible says. The National Conference of Catholic Bishops has said, "The scriptures as we have them today were written over a long period of time and reflect many varied historical situations, all different from our own. Our understanding of them is both complicated and enhanced by these differences, but not in any way obscured or diminished by them."[17] Differences make a difference. Biblical interpretation ought to take these differences into consideration. The Bible reflects the ancient cultures and world views in which it was written. There are many biblical texts that are problematic in contemporary culture, especially texts that speak of the ownership of other people, whether the ownership of slaves or the ownership of women by men. Lisa Sowle Cahill suggests that interpreters must make judgments about which texts are more culturally bound and thus less central in contrast to texts that are essential or authoritative for contemporary Christian moral reflection.[18] While agreeing that context makes a difference, other commentators are concerned about such proposals. Hays writes, for example, "The effort to distinguish timeless truth in the New Testament from culturally conditioned elements is wrong-headed and impossible."[19] Hays suggests "three focal images," namely community, cross, and new creation, through which to interpret the

New Testament. Both authors are giving an account of interpretive principles, principles used both to govern the selection of texts as well as the significance of texts. Interpretors must be clear about their operative interpretive principles.

Third, the hermeneutical task defends the notion that God's revelation is present through the Bible. The Bible is the primary source for Christian moral reflection. As "the privileged . . . source of our knowledge of God and God's intentions for us,"[20] the Bible confronts us and challenges us to "reshape our perceptions of ourselves, our communities, our faith and our moral relationships."[21] That is, the Bible has "the power to speak to us who have new questions and a new context of understanding."[22]

This approach holds that the meaning of the text today can transcend its face value. In the words of Stanley Hauerwas, "Scripture is capable of unanticipated relevancy through reinterpretation."[23] To use an often quoted phrase, the Bible has "an excess of meaning." Brown and Schneiders write, "The Bible is God's word to audiences of all time. This continuing biblical engagement of readers/hearers with God uncovers meaning beyond that envisioned by the human author in his local and limited circumstances."[24] William Spohn speaks of "analogical reasoning" in biblical interpretation. Persons of faith can reflect on the correspondence between the biblical story and their personal context. The narrative then serves as a basis for understanding their situation. He writes, "The biblical story enables us to recognize *which* features of experience are significant, guides *how* we act, and forms *who* we are in the community of faith."[25]

Fourth, the task of biblical interpretation presupposes that the Bible does not contain the fullness of God's revelation. Primary does not mean exclusive. The Bible is one of the means through which we presently discern God's will.[26] The ground for this position is the Christian belief that the revelation of God is not a once-and-for-all thing. God's presence, God's love continues to be revealed in and through the world. If this is the case, then the role of the Bible is clarified and, to an extent, relativized. For Christians the Bible is not merely a text conveying ancient wisdom. God's revelation continues through the Bible within human history. The Bible "is" the word of God in the present tense. As such it needs to be read and understood within the context in which the reader belongs.

With this section on methodology as background, we will now explore two crucial biblical narratives. These stories, in differing ways, describe the relationships between people and God. The first, the image of God theme from Genesis, chapter 1, tells us something about the nature of persons. The second, the Exodus story, tells us something about the nature of God. Both stories serve as foundations for understanding the biblical imperative of justice.

HUMANS: CREATED IN THE IMAGE OF GOD

The first few chapters of the Bible are loaded with interesting and surprising features. For many Christians, the most startling thing about these short chapters is that they contain two separate and distinct stories of creation. The first Creation story starts with the famous, "In the beginning" and narrates the seven days that culminate with the creation of humanity late on the sixth day. This narrative is told in Genesis 1–2:4a. The second story of creation contains the often repeated story of Adam and Eve in the Garden of Eden. It is found in Genesis 2:4b–25. One theory to explain this phenomenon suggests that the reason we have two creation stories in the Bible is the stories themselves predate the Bible. When the biblical authors, or better stated, biblical editors, compiled the early books in the Bible, they drew from the existing oral narrative traditions of the community. They had to include two stories because there were two within the community.

The Story

The author of the first story, referred to by biblical scholars as the "P" source, presents us with an orderly, developmental, and systematic presentation of the creation of the cosmos. From the perspective of this work, two ideas stand out. The first is that all of creation—light and darkness, the sky, earth and sea, stars and sun, birds, fish and animals—springs forth from the very word of God. On each day, the text says, "God said" and creation spontaneously occurs. The second point is related. The narrator comments that after each creative act, with the exception of the second day, "God saw that it was good." The goodness of all creation—water, earth, sky, every plant and animal— rests on the fact of its divine origin. It is all good before the creation of humans. This gives us some insight into the moral value of creation. All of creation, everything in creation, has an intrinsic value. That is to say, the goodness of creation rests in its very nature. The goodness of creation rests in the fact that God created it, not that it is good for humans.

The first story of creation culminates on the seventh day, the Sabbath. This day of rest follows the creation of humans. God's creative activity seems to move from the more fundamental and basic elements to the more complex parts of creation. Thus on that final day, God first creates the wild animals, cattle and all the creatures that creep on the ground, and then, in a separate creative act, God creates humans. The author here clearly wants to communicate an exalted view of humans.[27] The climax of the narrative is the creation of humans. In case the reader misses this in the text, the author stresses this three times in the description of humanity. First, three times in two verses, we read of God's creating humans in God's own image. This creation is not of a single person, as is found in the second story of creation. Here, God creates male and female together, in the same creative moment. Indeed the text associates the image of God with the creation of man and woman, not with the creation of individuals. Second, humans or humankind are said to be created in God's "likeness." Third, the author states that humans are created with "dominion" over the rest of creation. The author ends this part of the narrative with yet another affirmation of the goodness of creation (the seventh time in the chapter) by telling us that God looked at all of creation and saw "it was very good."

The phrase the "image of God" has a dominant place in these few verses of the first chapter of Genesis. It has also had an important role in the history of Christian theological and moral reflection. But it is interesting to note that the theme has no prominence in the later parts of the Old Testament. In the whole of the Old Testament, the theme of persons being created in the image of God occurs only four times. Of the thirty-nine books in the Hebrew Scriptures, it occurs twice, both times in Genesis (1:26 and 9:6). The other two times can be found in the Apocryphal/Deuterocanonical Books of Sirach and Wisdom of Solomon. In the other Genesis verse, 9:6, the image of God theme affirms the exalted place of humans within creation. It defends the dignity of human life against the violent tendencies of the age, as it condemns murder and warns of God's retribution for such violence. The other two texts, Wisdom of Solomon 2:23–24 and Sirach 17:1–3, echo Genesis 1:26 and affirm God granting humans authority and the related power over the earth.

The theme of the "image of God" or divine image occurs a number of times in the New Testament. However, its use is fundamentally different from its use in the Old Testament. While there is at least one occasion where it is referred to in reference to humanity (James 3:9), and one passage where it seems to refer to men and not women (1 Cor 11:7), its usage is not so much anthropological as it is soteriological. That is, the primary use of the "image of God" theme in the New Testament is not to describe the essential features or characteristics of humanity. The New Testament writers are not so much interested in common features of humanity as they are with the salvation of humans. There are two ways the "image of God" theme is used in a soteriological context in the New Testament. The first is in reference to who Jesus is. Several times the texts refer to Jesus as "the image of the invisible God" (Col 1:15; see also 2 Cor 4:4). This phrase is not used here to indicate a general description of humanity, but rather a description of a particular person. Describing Jesus as the "image of God" indicates His intimate and unique relationship to God, and it is through Jesus that we gain salvation, thus the second use of the theme. Christians ought to "put on" the "image of God," namely Jesus. This second use of the theme then in the New Testament describes the appropriate actions and attitudes of believers (Col 3:10).

Overall, both the New Testament and the Old Testament present a more ambiguous view of human nature than simply that humans are in the "image of God." While, for example, Psalm 8 proclaims that humans are crowned with glory and honor and indeed are created just a bit lower than God, other passages are not so certain of human goodness. One of the characters in the Book of Job exclaims, for example, "Human beings are born to trouble, just as sparks fly upward" (Job 5:6–7). What this suggests is that the first chapter of Genesis cannot be read apart from the third chapter, the disobedience of Adam and Eve and God's curse. Here God reminds the man that he will return to the dust in the ground from which he was originally created.

Some have argued that the "image of God" theme is not a particularly helpful theological concept because it rests on circular reasoning. Humans, a critic might suggest, always describe God by qualities that are highly regarded in their cultures. Loving, for example, is one of the greatest things a person can do for another, thus if God is the greatest being, God must be loving. To say then that humans are the image and likeness of God is to merely rebound the human categories ascribed to God back down to humans.

This is a significant critique, and perhaps there is no way around it. But we cannot speak of God, or any other reality, apart from our experience, either personal, collective, or historical. Our understanding of God and God's activity through history emerges out of our very experience. There is no way to detach human nature from human experience. Thus we use human words and human experiences to understand God. However, if we are seeking a sense of what it means to be a person, if we are trying to make some anthropological claims based on the "image of God" idea, then we have to admit that such claims would ultimately be based on a faith statement. You have to believe in God to say that people are created in the "image of God." Indeed the context of the Genesis text affirms this. Like the Creation accounts in Genesis, chapters 1 and 2, the statement that persons are created in the "image of God" is more of a confession of faith than an empirical or scientific inquiry.[28] The critique that the concept is illogical because it is based on circular thinking does not nullify using the concept.

God's Stand-Ins

The history of commentary on the meaning of the "image of God" in the Christian theological tradition is rich and descriptive. Commentators and theologians have tended to link the concept with a particular feature of human nature. For example, many have described the image of God as residing in the immortal soul of persons. Others have suggested it lies in human freedom or human intellect or that humans are moral actors (that is to say that humans have the ability to act with freedom and knowledge). Other explanations of the "image of God" theme look to the relational or social nature of persons, or that persons have a spiritual nature.[29] But what might the text have meant to the original community? Most biblical scholars state that the image of God in persons does not so much refer to a particular human feature as it does to the totality of human personhood and a particular human function. Except for the immortality of the soul, a concept foreign to ancient Jewish religion, all of the other interpretations, taken together, could describe the implications of this term. Yet the fullness of the term is not completely captured through the description of human characteristics. It is rather more fully understood through an understanding of human function.

The word used for "image" in this text refers to a symbolic representation of a king, either in the form of a statue or a viceroy.[30] A viceroy is a person appointed by a king or higher authority to rule over a province. The viceroy has the responsibility to rule the area as the king would rule the area. That is, the viceroy has to embody the king's values and goals. It is important to note that the source of the viceroy's authority comes from the king, not from the viceroy himself. The viceroy serves the king. According to Jon Levenson, it was characteristic of ancient Near East civilizations to see their king as their god's viceroy on earth. What we have in the Genesis text then is a dramatic democratization of this idea. Genesis 1:26 says that humans, all humans, are God's viceroys on earth. Levenson writes, "it appoints the entire human race as God's royal stand-in."[31] Humans are charged with the responsibility to ensure that God's values and goals are actualized. The earth is "ours" in the same way that a viceroy would claim responsibility and dominion, not ownership, over the province. Humans can never truly own the earth. Humans are responsible, however, to God and responsible for the earth and the rest of creation. The exalted view of humans advocated in this narrative then does not serve to justify the superiority of humans in the world, but rather to propose a view of human responsibility in the world.

This understanding of the "image of God" has important implications for how we are to understand the word "dominion." The connotation of this Latin–based term used to translate the original Hebrew is very strong. To us it suggests an overriding and indeed supreme authority over something, perhaps even a tyrannical authority. But this meaning clearly does not follow from the text. While "some degree of domination of nature is necessary" by humans, agricultural cultivation in this sense is a domination of nature, the fuller meaning of the text must be understood within the vision that persons are God's representatives.[32] The Wisdom of Solomon illustrates this theme in a reference to human dominion, i.e., to "rule the world in holiness and righteousness" (Wis 9:3).[33]

I stated above that one cannot read Genesis, chapters 1 and 2, without reading chapter 3. Genesis, chapter 3, narrates human disobedience to God and the consequences of this disobedience. Nowhere, however, does it say that the image of God is wiped out or that it is hidden or blurred because of this disobedience. In fact, the consequences of sin illustrate even more the need to recognize the role of responsibility. One can argue that much of the Bible narrates the tension between

Genesis, chapter 1, and Genesis, chapter 3: God continually expects humans to be responsible (indeed it is part of being human), but often humans are not as responsible as God expects them to be. Being created in the "image of God" makes it possible for God to direct questions to people and indeed for humans to question themselves and God. For example, in chapter 3 God asks the man, "Where are you?" The man is expected to respond and he does. He tells God that he is hiding because he is naked. God asks him about the source of his new–found knowledge. Did he eat the fruit? The man, in a brazen attempt to deny personal responsibility, first blames God for creating the woman and then he blames the woman for giving him the fruit! We are created in the "image of God," we are to be God's viceroys on earth, yet we do not always recognize the depth of our responsibility. The most compelling illustration of this is found in Genesis chapter 4. After Cain killed Abel, God asks Cain where his brother is, and Cain denies not only his guilt but also his "image of God." He responds in that often quoted statement, "Am I my brother's keeper?"[34] Even today this sarcastic comment underscores responsibility, to God and for others, as the heart of the moral life.

Implications

The Bible begins with a narrative, a story. That story tells us what is at stake in life. It tells us about God and it tells us about people. It, moreover, describes a relationship between God and people. In doing so, it sets up the conditions for the possibility of the moral life. We are called . . . sometimes we do not listen. This simple story is much more powerful than a philosophical treatise on human nature.

Reflection on the "image of God" in the creation texts gives us some insight into the more general issue of using the Bible in contemporary ethics. The reason for this is that while Genesis 1–3 has important implications for Christian moral reflection, it does not substantively address the two fundamental questions of the moral life, "Who am I to be?" and "What am I to do?" This is because the first chapters of the Bible are more "descriptive" than "prescriptive." That is, they do not give directives regarding the questions of being and doing; they do, however, attempt to describe important aspects of the reality of the human condition. The purpose of the "image of God" text is not to give us a picture of the moral life. The moral import of this text is that it provides a frame for the picture of the moral life. It is, after all, a narrative. There are no rules here nor are there detailed descriptions of virtues. Genesis, chapter 1, tells as that we are God's representatives. Another way of describing this is to say these Genesis texts provide a "revealed reality" more than a "revealed morality."[35] That is, they describe part of the framework within which Christian moral reflection ought to work, specifically, an anthropology (an understanding of what it means to be a human) and a vision of God as the ultimate source of creation.

What then is the reality revealed in the "image of God" text? The text indicates that we, God's stand-ins on earth, are multidimensional and have a relational nature as well as an individual nature. The very being of a person is bound to his or her relationship to God, to other persons, and to nature. As God's responsible representatives, "the creative ordering of the world has become something that humanity can not only witness and celebrate, but something in which it can also take part."[36] This all suggests the following:

1) Humans are social beings. The destiny of every person is bound with the lives of many other persons. Indeed, as Genesis 1:26 states, the "Image of God" is in the male and female together.

2) Humans are a part of creation; not separate from, but in relation to, creation. Humans have the responsibility to protect and maintain the earth as God would protect and maintain the earth. Humans, moreover, are not the sole bearers of intrinsic value.[37] The goodness of creation, according to the text, preceded the creation of persons.

3) Humans are responsible. Each person, like the man and woman in the second creation story, is responsible to God. Each person is responsible for one's actions. Each person is responsible for other people.

4) There is an essential equality among humans. The "image of God" in persons is not based on the character of the individual. The "image of God" is prior to individual merit, achievement, social status, race, gender, economic resources, or any other nonessential aspect of the person. It is the "image of God" that is the essential aspect of persons. This affirmation has significant moral implications for issues of human equality as well as for the exalted view, or sacredness, of persons.

These four points are the foundations for a Christian interpretation of justice. Persons, you and I, people in power and people who are vulnerable, are social, related to creation, responsible, and fundamentally equal.

THE EXODUS

The Book of Genesis is about origins: origins of the cosmos and the world, of human beings, of sin, of the people Israel through stories of its ancestors.[38] The second book of the Bible, the Book of Exodus, is also about origins. Exodus, the book and the event, is the story of the birth of the Israelites as the community of the people of God. As such it is also the story of the ancient beginning of the Christian community.[39]

God Stands against Evil

The importance of the Exodus for us is that it furthers our examination into the frameworks of a biblically based understanding of justice. If Genesis describes a creator God, Exodus describes a God who liberates and sustains. Exodus, moreover, details the appropriate response of the community to this God. These events, the liberation from Egypt and the covenant making on Mount Sinai, have been referred to as the "root experiences" of Israel's religious tradition.[40]

The importance of the Exodus event in the context of the Bible and the subsequent Jewish and Christian faiths cannot be overestimated. Bruce Birch argues that in reading the Bible, one finds the "continued testimony to the meaning and importance of the Exodus event as the focus of Israel's understanding of itself in relation to God."[41] Gustavo Gutierrez suggests, "The memory of the Exodus pervades the pages of the Bible."[42] It is the foundational story in the Old Testament. "All Jewish tradition reaches back to" the experiences of the Exodus and the covenant "which constitute the people's basic understanding of their own identity and the identity and character of God."[43] The meaning overflows from the Old Testament into the New Testament offering Christians from the first century interpretive tools that have helped to make sense of the life and death of Jesus.

Pattern of Faith

The meaning of this narrative, however, does not simply lie in the past. God's liberating concern through the Exodus is not a one-time event nor is it an isolated event. God's liberating concern is a dominant and reoccurring experience in the history of salvation. The Exodus event has become a paradigmatic lens through which persons of faith (and indeed, as Michael Waltzer has suggested, the Western world) have come to interpret their own stories and the narratives of their own people. The meaning, authority, and significance of the narrative come not only from the fact of its place in Scripture but of its confirmation in the lives of believers through the ages. Our God is a liberating God, a God who stands against evils of injustice, oppression, and exploitation, a God who, in the words of Jesus' mother Mary, brings down the powerful and lifts up the lowly (Luke 1:52). Bruce Birch suggests that a paradigmatic pattern of faith has emerged based on the Exodus. This pattern, repeated within the Bible and the history of the church, includes three distinct stages: 1) a situation of distress, 2) an unexpected deliverance, and 3) a response in community.[44] Let's review the Exodus event through these categories.

The situation of distress: The story begins (see Exodus 1–2) with a concise but graphic description of oppression. The pharaoh of Egypt is depicted in an almost god-like role controlling every aspect of the Israelites' lives. The Israelites, captive foreigners, live in a "land of slavery" under brutal, repressive, and dehumanizing conditions (including a policy of infanticide aimed at controlling their population). Although Exodus records how some women actively tried to subvert the repression, the people are beaten into subservience. They seem unable to liberate themselves. Resistance is futile and is continually met with harsher measures (Exodus 5). An interesting feature here is that the people are not particularly religious. They do not do anything to deserve God's attention or intervention. Yet God heard them as they cried out in misery.

The story then begins with a clear picture. The people live under atrocious conditions. Such conditions encourage us to ask questions to understand the story. For example, is it by chance that the people live in these conditions? Is the cause of their misfortune a natural disaster, such as a famine or a flood? Is it simply unfortunate that the people find themselves in this position? Are they then unlucky? Is the situation a direct result of their choosing and willing? Did they simply make a bad decision and are facing the consequences? Did they deserve to live this way? Is it their fault? Are they being punished for some wrong that they have done? The text indicates a strong "no" to all these questions. The situation of the people described in the first chapters of Exodus is not simply one of misfortune or desert. It is one of injustice. They are being "wronged" through the direct and free willing of the pharaoh. Indeed there is a whole system, based on the acquiescence of people all along the way, that oppresses them. The story starts with injustice, and this is where considerations of justice ought to begin. We can start to form the abstract considerations of justice from reflection on concrete experiences of injustice.[45]

The unexpected deliverance: It was within these conditions that Moses was called by God to mediate between God and the people and God and the pharaoh (Exodus 3–4). Liberation does not come easily, even if God is the liberator. Moses is reluctant to follow God's plans. He even tries to talk his way out of becoming involved. He is ultimately unsuccessful in refusing God and finds he is, at first, unsuccessful doing what God wants. Pharaoh is not moved by Moses' words. It takes ten terrible plagues sent by God to persuade the pharaoh to let the people go (Exodus 7–13). Yet even then, following the awful destruction and death of the Passover, the pharaoh changes his mind and chases the Israelites to the sea. It is there that he and his army meet military defeat in the rushing waters (Exodus 14). The exploited, oppressed, and helpless people are liberated by the one God. The God who is not limited by the powers of others nor tied to a specific location. Moses is the unlikely mediator, and the people are unlikely candidates for God's intervention.

The response in community: It is interesting that God does not save individuals in this story. God liberates a people who then form a community. This saving/liberating act is clearly a social and a political act. God does not merely free people from their mental anguish or spiritual sufferings. The Exodus is not about God freeing people from their own sin. As God frees people from "that land of slavery," God frees them from the sinful actions of others. This is an important point that must not be lost. It is difficult to spiritualize and privatize the Exodus event. The Exodus is the story not only of liberation, but of the liberator. God is on the side of freedom. God is on the side of justice. A moral imperative follows from this truth. Corresponding to this understanding of God is an expectation of people. If God is on the side of justice and hears the powerless, so too should the followers of God.

The thoroughly social nature of the Exodus, however, has personal ramifications. Individuals are not lost in the collective society. Persons are rather called to be responsible and responsive to others in the society. The Exodus is described as the birth of the community in that through this new-found relationship with God, the people must redirect their understanding of their relations with others. The liberating act of

God requires that people establish justice amongst themselves. The place of the Ten Commandments in the Book of Exodus attests to this.

In the Book of Exodus, Moses receives the Ten Commandments, along with other laws in the Covenant Code on Mount Sinai soon after the Israelites are freed from Egypt (Exodus 20–23). After living all those years under the pharaoh who defined reality and the social ordering for the Israelites, the Covenant Code establishes a new reality and social ordering under the guidance of God. The first line of the Ten Commandments reads like a preface to the laws that follow. It illustrates the new relation between the liberating God and the moral community. It reads, "I am the Lord your God, who brought you out of the land of Egypt, out of the house of slavery; you shall have no other gods before me" (Exodus 20: 2–3).

There is a reciprocal relationship between justice in the community and worship in the Book of Exodus. The structure of the Ten Commandments illustrates this as does the structure of the Book of Exodus itself. The first three commandments concern the people's relation to God. The final six refer to relationships within the community. Morality is the expected response to God. The proclamation of the moral laws, on the other hand, precede the proclamation of the ritual laws and the establishment of the Tabernacle at the end of Exodus. "The ordering of society is, in a sense, a prerequisite for the creation of a worshipping community."[46]

Implications

As a paradigmatic event, the Exodus event calls for a dialogue between the particulars of the story and the particulars of the contemporary experiences of the reader. Persons of faith ought to reflect on the correspondence between the biblical story and their personal context. The Exodus can serve as a basis for understanding their situation. Recall William Spohn's discussion of analogical reasoning. Analogical reasoning discerns resemblance as well as difference between contemporary experience and Scripture. It may give us insight into our experience but does not tell us exactly what to do in a particular context.

Martin Luther King Jr. provides us with an interesting example of the analogical use of the Exodus story. In his telling of the narrative of civil rights, he refers to Abraham Lincoln and the Emancipation Proclamation. While the Emancipation Proclamation brought African-

Americans "nearer to the Red Sea, it did not guarantee . . . passage through the parted waters." He continues:

> In the great struggle of the last half century between the forces of justice attempting to end the evil system of segregation and the forces of injustice attempting to maintain it, the pharaohs have employed legal maneuvers, economic reprisals, and even physical violence to hold the Negro in the Egypt of segregation. Despite the patient cry of many a Moses, they refused to let the Negro people go.[47]

The key point of contact mediating the Exodus event and any hermeneutical work (contemporary interpretation) is the directive role that the oppressed play. The theme that God hears the cries of the powerless, whether described as the oppressed, the poor, the widow, the orphan, or the stranger in the land, is enduring throughout the Bible and the Jewish and Christian traditions. It is this special concern for the powerless that forms one of the basic elements of a biblically informed understanding of justice. We will see this theme repeated in the next sections on prophets and Jesus.

The Creation story and the Exodus are foundational narratives for a contemporary Christian understanding of justice. As stories of origin, both address the classic questions of identity, that is, who are we? The "image of God" theme offers profound insight into the human condition. We are responsible representatives of God. The Exodus gives us insight into this God in whose image we are. Our God is the God of justice who listens to the cries of the powerless. The Creation stories and the Exodus also serve to inspire persons of faith. Being created as God's responsible representatives is an awesome call. Both Adam and Eve, as well as Cain, could not live up to such responsibility. But the challenge remains. We are, moreover, children of the Exodus. These stories are normative for us. As such they give us direction through the myriad of narratives we hear every day. They invite us to challenge what we hear in our culture and through our media about being human and human responsibility.

CHAPTER TWO

God Has Told You What Is Good

> But let justice roll down like waters, and righteousness like
> an ever-flowing stream.
>
> —Amos 5:24

THE EIGHTH CENTURY PROPHETS

Some of the most interesting and compelling reading in the Bible is the prophets. The biblical use of the term "prophet" describes persons throughout both the Hebrew and Christian Scriptures who mediate and interpret God's will. Moses, Aaron, and Miriam, for example, are called prophets in the Book of Exodus. Jesus, John the Baptist, and a host of persons Luke mentions in the Acts of the Apostles are referred to as prophets in the Christian Scriptures. These people are messengers for God. The paradigmatic form of the prophet and prophecy is set by the so called "classical prophets." These prophets, who lived between the eighth and sixth centuries B.C. or B.C.E., are the subject of books in the Hebrew Bible. The list of these includes, Amos, Hosea, Isaiah, Micah, Nahum, Zephanian, Habakuk, Jeremiah, and Ezekiel. The form and indeed the content of the prophecy of the classical prophets has inspired a distinct form of contemporary moral discourse.

Like the previous chapter, this chapter will describe a particular form of moral discourse and biblical texts relating this form to justice. This chapter will, however, reverse the discussion. As contemporary prophetic discourse is modeled on prophetic discourse in the Bible, the biblical texts will be examined first. Not all the biblical prophets will be considered here. For the present purposes, we will look only at the earliest of them, namely, the eighth century prophets Amos, Hosea, Micah, and Isaiah, chapters 1–39, known as "First Isaiah" or "Isaiah of Jerusalem."[1] Although there are important differences among the four prophets, they are united in their concern for justice. Both their message and their style are significant for contemporary concerns about justice.

After reviewing the eighth century prophets, we will consider prophetic discourse in the modern world.

One of the first things to remember as we look to the prophets as a source for wisdom in our task to develop a contemporary Christian understanding of justice is that prophets are not philosophers. For philosophers, the rules of logic, coherence, and consistency dominate the discourse. Philosophers tend to speak in abstractions and often are as interested in discussing method and justification as they are in conclusions. Many philosophers think in terms of universals. They work to discern universal truth and universal propositions. The vocation of the philosopher is very different from the calling of the prophet. The prophets, though they passionately speak against injustice, offer us no concrete definition of justice. They certainly are more provocative and more loose with language than your average philosopher. Gerhard von Rad states that the prophet "uses even the most suspect means to tie the listening partner down to his particular time and place in order to make him understand his own situation before God."[2] When one reads the words of a prophet, one does not hear "perennial religious truth, but a message addressed to a specific moment in history."[3] Prophets address concrete historical circumstances and the lives of particular people, and it must be noted that the moment addressed by the eighth century prophets was twenty-eight centuries ago! The methods and purpose of the prophets then point us in a certain direction for interpretation. When we read the prophets we have to remember the extraordinary cultural differences between ancient Israel and our lives. We have to remember that their words were directed toward a specific community. At the same time, we can ask ourselves how our society seems like the society in which the prophets lived. We can examine the prophetic indictments and consider if we too are guilty of the same or similar crimes. The links between cultures may be our common humanity and our common quest to know and serve God.

Conscience of the Community

The earliest of the eighth century prophets, Amos, appears some seven hundred years after the Exodus. Much had happened during that time. The descendants of the slaves had become a nation. They had long split into two kingdoms, Israel in the North and Judah in the South and had had an endless list of kings, including the famous Kings David and Solomon. The development of the monarchy had both positive and negative features. Before the monarchy and its hierarchical structure of organization, the people were organized in and through twelve tribes. These tribes had systems of mediation, collaboration, and hierarchy. While this was beneficial for internal relations, it was not an efficient structure for external relations. If Israel was to stand among the nations and provide an adequate defense against its aggressive neighbors, it needed a unified political structure. It needed a king. The monarchy, while perhaps a necessary feature of social organization in that world, was always under scrutiny by the prophets. The structure as well as the individual king could never fully capture the rich moral vision of the prophets.

The eighth century prophets saw two threats to Israel's well-being, one internal and the other external. Israel was experiencing a time of economic prosperity. This prosperity, however, was not equitable. It came with a price, and the price was a growing burden on the poor and powerless. One way to think of the prosperity, in contemporary economic terms, is to say that the Gross National Product (GNP) of the land was rising while the conditions of the poor and powerless in the land became desperate. Thus a consistent theme of our four prophets is economic justice. They addressed questions of fairness as well as how the wealth was generated. The prosperity allowed the leaders and the rich social elite to have a sense of complacency. In their minds, things were going just fine. All the while a neighboring nation, Assyria, was preparing for its eventual conquest of Israel. The prophets saw both the danger that Assyria posed and the moral problems that characterized this prosperity. Indeed the prophets saw the internal and external threats as one. The social reality the prophets saw was that the people had broken their covenant with God. The people had not been faithful to God. They ignored their ancient law and historical relationship with God.

The prophets indict the people on two counts. First, they argue the leaders and rich elite have systematically oppressed the powerless. This was, in their minds, an affront to the holiness of God.[4] Second, they condemn the people for their rejection of their exclusive relationship with God. The people were guilty of practicing pagan religious beliefs, the most prominent being Baalism. People attributed fertility and their harvest to Baal. The cult of Baal included sexual activity. "Its rationale, briefly stated, was the belief that human sexual activity in a sacred place could stimulate divine sexual action and thereby foster fertility and prosperity throughout the natural realm."[5] Thus the prophets believed that the military threat that Assyria posed was nothing more than God's response to the unfaithful people. As Thomas Ogletree narrates, "If Jerusalem is in danger because of foreign military moves, that danger is in any case Yahweh's own doing, his visitation in judgment. The people have no need, therefore, to fear Damascus or Samaria, not even Assyria; it is Yahweh whom they need to fear."[6]

As the conscience of the community, the mission of the prophet was to hold a mirror to the face of the community and force the people to look at themselves. Their identity, their self-understanding was based on their relationship to God known through the tradition of narratives. The prophets spoke within the frame of the long and storied history of the people. Though by no means conservative, the prophets looked back and brought the wisdom from the tradition to bear on the current historical context. Some prophets, like Amos, were outsiders; others, like Isaiah, came from within the royal court. They knew that God was now acting in their midst just as God had acted in the Creation and in the Exodus. Birch states, "Although God's word may be known through the traditions of the past, the prophets believed in the power of God's words to change history for the future."[7]

The Message of the Prophets

To enter the minds of the prophets is an exciting and challenging quest. Their overpowering moral vision cannot but force us to reconsider our moral lives. This section will offer a brief consideration of these prophets. As you read these few pages, try to pull yourself into the prophets' words and see the world as they saw the world. The way you see the world might never be the same. We will consider the four prophets in their historical order: Amos, Hosea, Isaiah of Jerusalem, and Micah.

Amos

As the Book of Amos begins, we hear the prophet speaking for God to the people of Israel. His words are strong and direct. Through Amos, God delivers an indictment against each of Israel's neighbors. One can imagine Amos' audience getting larger and drawing nearer to him as he accuses the rival nations of terrible crimes against humanity. His hearers were perhaps nodding their heads in affirmation and cheering Amos. After citing the sins of Damascus, Gaza, Tyre, Edom, the Ammonites, Moab, and Judah, Amos turns his attention and his words on Israel. What has Israel done wrong? "Thus says the Lord: For three transgressions of Israel, and for four, I will not revoke the punishment; because they sell the righteous for silver, and the needy for a pair of sandals—they trample the heads of the poor into the dust of the earth and push the afflicted out of the way" (Amos 2:6–7). Note the corporate and social nature of the indictment. Individuals, whether the oppressed or the oppressors, are not mentioned.

Amos condemns a dominant social practice or a characteristic pattern of social relations. People, good people, are being trampled upon by the rich and powerful. People, impoverished by the policies of the elite, are forced "to sell their land and even themselves . . . for the trifling sum" of a pair of sandals.[8] This is a scandal. These people are the people who based their very identity in liberation of their ancestors from slavery. The land on which they lived and which granted them full citizenship was thought to be from God through their ancestors. Now their own people were forcing them to be landless and slaves. The former victims of slavery were acting like their oppressors within their own culture. The king and the rich elite of Israel renewed the pharaoh's oppression against their own people. The dominant emotion one hears in the Book of Amos is anger, righteous anger. God is furious. "Hear this word that the Lord has spoken against you, O people of Israel, against the whole family that I brought up out of that land of Egypt: You only have I known of all the families of the earth; therefore I will punish you for all your iniquities" (Am 3:1–2).

Within these quotations we see both the strong passionate language of the prophet as well as an indication of the depth of the prophetic critique. As if forcing poverty and slavery upon one's fellow community members were not enough, Amos continues his list of crimes. "Hear this, you that trample on the needy, and bring to ruin the poor of the land, saying [when will the Sabbath be over?] so that we may offer wheat for sale; and practice deceit with false balances, buying the poor for silver and the needy for a pair of sandals" (Am 8:5). The indictment rings of irony here. Amos describes the people as living two separate lives. One part of their lives was "religious." They performed their ritual obligations quite well. They observed the required Sabbath and holy day obligations in exemplary form. Yet they were religious failures. How could this be? For Amos and the other prophets, worship without morality, prayer without justice, was of no value. In biting sarcasm Amos mocks those who sin on one day and perform their religious obligations the next (Am 4:4). It is interesting to note that Amos does not accuse them of hypocrisy. The people are so blinded by their sin that they do not even know they are sinning! In the above quote, we hear about business people eager for the holy day to end so they could get back to work and profit from cheating people. They are fools because they do not understand the depth of real commitment to God.

The list of crimes continues. "For I know how many are your transgressions, and how great are your sins—you who afflict the righteous, who take a bribe, and push aside the needy in the gate. Therefore the prudent will keep silent in such a time; for it is an evil time" (Am 5:12–13). The city gate was the center for the administration of justice, and the integrity of that institution was at risk. Amos decries the rich who hate this traditional social practice because it "restricts their ability to defraud the poor."[9] He also condemns immoral administrators who make decisions on the basis of money and the social status of the person. They ignore the valid claims of the powerless. Amos states that the wise person keeps silent during these times, perhaps fearing for his own well-being. His indictment of Israel also includes the crime of complacency. Amos denounces the idle rich who lounge in luxurious settings, drink fine wine and eat delicacies (Am 6:4–7). He also targets the demanding wives of the rich whom he refers to as cows (Am 4:1).

Through ironic words he captures the readers' imagination. Elsewhere in the Hebrew Scriptures we hear of God's love for justice (see Ps(s) 33:5, 37:28, 99:4) and know that justice is something to be desired and longed for. Later generations will speak, for example, of a hunger for justice and righteousness. For Amos, the "justice" of Israel was not something sweet or something to be desired. The prevailing social notion of justice stood in sharp contradiction to the justice of God. He assails the people for turning "justice into poison" (Am 6:12) and turning justice into wormwood, a bitter revolting plant (Am 5:7). There is little wonder why the prudent remain silent.

Amos' prescriptions, like his indictments, are strong and direct. "Seek me [God] and live" (Am 5:4). "Seek good and not evil" (Am 5:14). "Hate evil and love good, and establish justice in the gate" (Am 5:15). "But let justice roll down like waters, and righteousness like and ever-flowing stream" (Am 5:24). There is, however, something dramatically different between the indictments and the prescriptions. The indictments are specific, relevant, and contextual. Amos was speaking to specific people and their specific practices. The prescriptions, on the other hand, are general and abstract. Compare, for example, the indictment "you who afflict the righteous, who take a bribe, and push aside the needy in the gate" with the prescription "Hate evil and love good." What is evidenced here is an attempt, a successful one at that, by the editor or an author of the Book of Amos to give the message of Amos a certain timelessness.[10] The abstract concepts of justice, righteousness, and good serve as something of a nexus around which the reader can understand his or her own time through a story that narrates events of two and a half millennia ago. The Book of Amos clearly makes a statement: One's relationship to God is dependent on one's relationship to other people. There is no separating what one "owes" to others and what one "owes" to God.

Hosea

The prophet Hosea is best known for his marriage to Gomer, a temple prostitute in the court of Baal. The union of Gomer and Hosea mirrors the union between God and Israel. Gomer, like Israel, unfaithful and guilty of many sins, leaves Hosea with three children whom he has presumably not fathered. Hosea's love and faithfulness as he waits for Gomer and welcomes her back give insight into the nature of God's love. Gomer has all but rejected her marriage covenant with Hosea, yet he remains steadfast in his commitment. Israel's sins, like Gomer's, are many. In a passage that echoes the Ten Commandments, Hosea declares, "Hear the word of the Lord, O people of Israel; for the Lord has an indictment against the inhabitants of the land. There is no faithfulness or loyalty, and no knowledge of God in the land. Swearing, lying, and murder, and stealing and adultery break out; bloodshed follows bloodshed" (Hos 4:1–2). Hosea seems particularly sensitive to the violence and war (Hos 1:4; 6:9; 10:13, 12:1). This is not the first biblical reference to God's displeasure over the violence. Genesis 6:11–13 cites the violence as God's reason for sending the flood.

The dominant word of Hosea, however, is not destruction or anger. Hosea describes God as one who reconciles anger and destruction with forgiveness. The dominant prophetic word here is love. "On that day, says the Lord . . . I will make a covenant . . . I will abolish the bow, the sword, and war from the land; and I will make you lie down in safety. I will take you for my wife in righteousness and in justice, in steadfast love, in mercy. I will take you for my wife in faithfulness; and you shall know the Lord" (Hos 2:16–20). Indeed in the remarkable eleventh chapter of the book, we read about this love of God in wonderful and moving language. The prophet describes God's enduring love portraying God as a parent. Throughout history God was there with the people, helping them, feeding them, feeling their joys and pains. God stood by as they rejected him, and could have punished them for their rebellion. Yet God's love is not like human love. In the face of their evil and their violence God responds, "My heart recoils within me: my compassion grows warm and tender" (Hos 11:8). In this passage, which has been called "one of the high points of the Old Testament revelation of God's nature,"[11] God's free love (Hos 14:4) prevails and the people will be brought back to full life.

Isaiah of Jerusalem

The cause of justice is foremost on the mind of the prophet Isaiah. Like the other prophets, Isaiah juxtaposes a description of the way things are with the way things ought to be. He begins with a commentary on the city of Jerusalem, the holy city, a symbol of the people and their identity. It is not a generous view! He forthrightly lambastes the people and their leaders. Like Hosea, he uses language of sexual infidelity and promiscuity to describe the lack of loyalty Israel has for God. "How the faithful city has become a whore! She that was full of justice, righteousness lodged in her—but now murderers! Your silver has become dross, your wine is mixed with water. Your princes are rebels and companions of thieves. Everyone loves a bribe and runs after gifts. They do not defend the orphan, and the widow's cause does not come before them" (Is 1:21–23). We have here a lament over the violence in society and the unjust administration of justice. The arbiters listen to money and not to the legitimate claims of the powerless. In a wonderful bit of sarcasm, Isaiah chides the leaders on the areas in which they really truly excel, "Ah, you who are heroes in drinking wine and valiant at mixing drink, who acquit the guilty for a bribe, and deprive the innocent of their rights!" (Is 5:23).

The passionate language continues as the indictment reveals a deeper level of moral culpability. On occasion, Isaiah uses the analogy of a vineyard to represent the people. In the following two quotations, he rebukes the leaders. "It is you who have devoured the vineyard; the spoil of the poor is in your houses. What do you mean by crushing my people, by grinding the face of the poor? says the Lord God of hosts" (Is 3:14–15). "For the vineyard of the Lord of hosts is the house of Israel, and the people of Judah are his pleasant planting; he expected justice, but saw bloodshed; righteousness, but heard a cry! Ah you who join house to house, who add field to field, until there is room for no one but you" (Is 5:7–8). The people, like grapes, are crushed beneath the greed of the rich. Here, Isaiah's concern is not how justice is administrated. What the people are doing is legal, but it is not moral. It is the promulgation of unjust laws that occasions the prophet's ire. "Ah, you who make iniquitous decrees, who write oppressive statutes, to turn aside the needy from justice and to rob the poor of my people of their right, that widows may be your spoil, and that you may make the orphans your prey!" (Is 10:1–2). Over a period of time, a systematic and legal procedure forced the poor from their land and their inheritance. The above passage "undoubtedly refers to those who foreclose the mortgages of the poor who cannot repay their debts, and turn their fields into their own personal property."[12]

What we have here is the stratification of society, the rich were getting richer and the poor were getting poorer, and, of course, the rich were building their wealth on the backs of the poor. As we heard in Amos, the oppressors continued to fulfill their ritual obligations, but God is repulsed by such acts. God will not listen to their prayers but rather commands them to "Wash yourselves; make yourselves clean; remove the evil of your doings from before my eyes; cease to do evil; learn to do good; seek justice, rescue the orphan, plead for the widow" (Is 1:16–17). The people can make themselves clean and pure by doing concrete acts of justice.

Micah

In Amos the leaders and social elite were said to trample the poor. In Isaiah they crush the poor. Here are the words of Micah: "And I said: Listen, you heads of Jacob and rulers of the house of Israel! Should you not know justice? you who hate the good and love the evil, who tear the skin off my people, and the flesh off their bones; who eat the flesh of my people, flay their skin off them, break their bones in pieces, and chop them up like meat in a kettle, like flesh in a caldron" (Mi 3:1–3). Micah describes the leaders as wild animals devouring the people. They are butchers and the people are nothing more than dead meat in their hands. By now we are familiar with the list of crimes. They include a moral distortion of the legal justice system. "Their hands are skilled to do evil; the official and the judge ask for a bribe, and the powerful dictate what they desire; thus they pervert justice" (Mi 7:3). It also includes a stinging indictment of business people. "The voice of the Lord cries to the city (it is sound wisdom to fear your name): Hear,

O tribe and assembly of the city! Can I forget the treasures of the wickedness in the house of the wicked, and the scant measure that is accursed? Can I tolerate wicked scales and a bag of dishonest weights? Your wealthy are full of violence; your inhabitants speak lies, with tongues of deceit in their mouths" (Mi 6:9–12). The leaders steal the land and inheritance of the people (Mi 2:2). No one in leadership positions is exempt from moral indictment. Even the priests and prophets are part of the conspiracy of injustice. "Hear this, you rulers of the house of Jacob and chiefs of the house of Israel, who abhor justice and pervert all equity, who build Zion with blood and Jerusalem with wrong! Its rulers give judgment for a bribe, its priests teach for a price, its prophets give oracles for money" (Mi 3:9–12).

Justice is not a passing theme for the eighth century prophets. It is a dominant part of their message and a critical element of moral discourse in the Hebrew Scriptures.

The Prophets on Justice

In our discussion of Genesis, chapter 1, and the "image of God" theme, it was suggested that the Creation stories offered us more of a "revealed reality" than a "revealed morality." That is, the "image of God" theme provides a description of persons as social, related to creation, responsible to God for others, and essentially equal. This frames an understanding of the moral life. It does not prescribe what we ought to do. We are God's responsible representatives, but there is no clear indication of how we should act. Genesis provides us with what might be called a "moral stance," a "moral position" in which we ought to see ourselves, a way we should "face" the world. The Exodus event includes both levels of moral conversation. It reveals the reality of God as a liberator who hears the cries of the poor. In the Covenant Code, which includes the Ten Commandments, we have revealed morality understood as the appropriate response to God. The prophets, in revealing God's will, also present a normative morality. They have a clear sense of right and wrong. The above section indicates that for Amos, Hosea, Isaiah, and Micah, justice was a dominant theme. The section also indicates what their central justice concern was: how the poor and powerless fared in the life of society.

The prophets offer us an expansive understanding of justice. Much of our contemporary public dialogue about justice is limited and concerns only one aspect of justice, namely, legal justice and the official administration of legal justice. Our most frequent use of the term then refers to justice in the courts. For example, after a trial we often ask, was justice served? Was the verdict just? Was the sentence fair (was the sentence just)? Did the defendant get what he deserved? Justice is served when the innocent go free and the evildoers are punished or forced to make some compensation or retribution for their crime. A key criterion for legal justice is objectivity. The often used symbol for legal justice, a blindfolded woman holding a balance or a scale, narrates the character-istics of this objectivity. Such justice does not grant favors to particular persons or groups. It treats like cases similarly. The blindfolded woman lets the balance take its natural course for an equitable relationship between the parties involved. The eighth century prophets often spoke of justice in this sense. They challenged the administration of legal justice on two grounds, bribery and partiality. Both practices were an affront to the law. The rich bribed the officials to make the "right decision," and the just claims of the poor and powerless were ignored. Indeed not only did the officials ignore the legitimate claims of the poor and those with no legal status, they had contempt for such persons.[13] The administrators perverted and poisoned justice. The symbolism of justice at the city gate is striking. People passed through the gate to get into the city. Thus people had to literally go through immorality to get to the city.

The prophets, however, did not simply equate justice with the appropriate administration of the law. In fact, the prophets did not even equate justice with the law. There is, at times, a tendency to blur the distinction between law and morality. Many people, today and during the time of the prophets, equate justice with the law. The thinking goes like this: If it is legal, it must be moral and just. The prophets, spurred by a moral vision much broader than the prevailing cultural and legal attitudes, rejected this view. They believed that the laws ought to be held up to the standard of justice. Thus they concluded that some laws were unjust. Christians concerned with justice through-out the ages have taken their cue from the prophets and have placed the laws of their own societies under moral scrutiny. Thomas Aquinas, for example, in the thirteenth century, presents a detailed analysis of law and the theory of law wherein he distinguishes just and unjust laws. Unjust laws, he says are "contrary to human good" and are "acts of violence rather than laws."[14] Aquinas tells us that we are not morally bound to follow such "laws." In our own time, Martin Luther King Jr. cites Aquinas as he condemns segregation laws. King writes, "A just

law is a man-made code that squares with the moral law or the law of
God. An unjust law is a code that is out of harmony with the moral
law. . . . Any law that uplifts human personality is just. Any law that
degrades human personality is unjust."[15] For the eighth century prophets,
the laws designed to expropriate land from the poor so as to increase
the wealth of the rich were acts of violence.

For the prophets, justice requires at least three types of action.
First, in reaction to the unfair court procedures, justice demands that
the leaders act to protect the interests of the powerless, whether through
equal protection under the law or equal treatment before the law.
Second, leaders must scrutinize the laws for their effect on the powerless.
Law plays a crucial role in society. If laws can be oppressive, they can
also be liberating. They can serve to give a sense of identity, purpose,
and meaning to a community. Unfortunately, the wickedness of the
rulers was personified through their unjust laws. Third, justice requires
appropriate social legislation aimed to protect the powerless against the
oppressive acts of the well-off. When the prophets refer to justice then
they mean "primarily that the officials and landowners should act on
behalf of the poor."[16]

Neither Amos, Hosea, Isaiah, nor Micah call for a revolution.
None call for the overthrow of the ruling system. In this sense, as in
others, they are not at all like Karl Marx who in his famous *Communist
Manifesto* declared: "The Communists . . . openly declare that their
ends can be attained only by the forcible overthrow of all existing social
conditions. Let the ruling classes tremble at a Communistic revolution.
The proletarians have nothing to lose but their chains."[17] While it might
be said that the prophets sought to free the people from the chains of
oppression, they are not social organizers. They do not seek to mobilize
the powerless into political groups. They do not call the poor to use
force to seek their ends. Indeed the violence of society was part of
their critique. Both Isaiah and Micah project the vision of the "peaceable
kingdom," time when the people will "beat their swords into plowshares
and, their spears into pruning hooks." That is, the people, under the
leadership of a messiah-king, will turn their weapons of destruction
into constructive farming tools. During this time, "nation shall not lift
up sword against nation, neither shall they learn war any more" (Is 2:4
and Mi 4:3). The overthrow of the social system or political structure
is not on the prophets' agenda; perhaps it is not within their imagination.

So what kind of change do these radicals call for? Donal Dorr
offers a helpful comment on social change. He suggests that the most

significant structures in society are not our cultural and economic systems but rather "our patterns of thinking and feeling and valuing." Dorr continues, "These are deeply personal; yet in many respects they transcend the individual. They are social realities which are often our unexamined presuppositions. They are 'within' the person without being private."[18] This is the insight of the prophets. The issue at hand for them is "the personal qualities, commitments, and convictions" of persons.[19] The call of the prophet was a call for conversion, yet it was not conversion in a narrow sense. In essence it was a call for liberation. It was a liberation characterized, in the words of Robert Inchausti, as "a personal transformation that leads the individual to aspire to a responsible life before God as opposed to a successful life within the cultural trance"[20] of greed, pride, and idolatry. Inchausti's phrase, "cultural trance" is striking. When persons are in a trance, they are unable to fully function. They are absorbed, hypnotized, in this context, by the trappings of culture. Walter Brueggemann argues the task of the prophets "is to nurture, nourish, and evoke a consciousness and perception alternative to the consciousness and perception of the dominant culture around us."[21] The prophets told the truth about this situation. This is why they were social outcasts; this is why the people often responded in anger to their message. The prophets were free from this cultural trance of the dominant culture that held captive the hearts and minds of the people and that well served the narrow interests of the ruling elite.

THE PROPHETIC FORM OF MORAL DISCOURSE

The legacy of the eighth century prophets is not only their expansive understanding of justice, it is their style, their form of moral communication. Recall the passionate words of the prophets. Have you ever heard any such words in contemporary society? Have you ever heard people speak out against environment degradation? Have you seen activists on the news preach against the 110 million land mines currently planted around the globe? Have you heard people decry the conditions of children in poverty? These people indict the dominant structures of society, whether the consumerism of rich countries, the military mentality and capitalistic ventures that produce and keep land mines, or gross inequalities and unjust distribution of the world's resources. Isaiah and Amos are among us. This brings us to a consideration of the second form of moral discourse, prophetic discourse. This distinctive style of moral communication, having its roots in the method of the eighth century prophets, is adapted to the modern world.

In the modern pluralistic world, prophets usually do not identify themselves as messengers from God. They do not usually begin their words speaking on behalf of God ("Thus says the Lord"), although some quote classic prophets. Contemporary prophets do, however, see themselves as the conscience of the community. Like the eighth century prophets, they are profoundly moved by justice, especially justice for the poor and vulnerable in society.

Conscience of the Community

The contemporary use of the term "prophet" primarily refers to one who foretells the future. While biblical prophets, and the prophetic mode of moral discourse that models it, might include a predictive element, foretelling the future is not a necessary or even a sufficient characterization of the prophet.[22] Rather, the prophet within the biblical tradition is one who acts as the conscience for the community. Commentators speak of two characteristics of the prophet or prophetic voice of moral discourse. The first is denunciation. The prophet pronounces an indictment of society denouncing its moral and social evils. The second is annunciation. The prophet proclaims the possibility of a new society, an alternative way to view reality and social relations, an alluring picture of the way things should be.

Prophetic Indictment

The prophet "tells the truth" about the way things are.[23] This truth-telling propels the prophet to offer a moral and religious indictment of the patterns of behavior within society or indeed of society itself. The prophet, in short, charges society and persons within society with a crime. This indictment usually has three typical features. First, the prophet publicly and comprehensively challenges persons and societies within the totality of their situation. Second, the charges against society are expressed in passionate and moving language. Third, the indictment as well as the prophet emerge from within the midst of the oppression or the evil being condemned.

The first outstanding characteristic of prophetic denunciation is that the prophet publicly and comprehensively challenges persons and societies. Although the prophet is a religious figure, the prophet's message is not limited to what we might think of as narrowly religious. Jon Sobrino, for example, writes that the prophetic message

> bears on the totality of secular, worldly history . . . on the totality of the life and death of men and women, on the relations of justice or injustice generated among them, on oppression and liberation. The strictly religious element of concrete life, while requiring explication, is not presented in authentic prophecy as an autonomous element parallel to the historical.[24]

The prophetic message is then not limited by a restrictive view of God's will and God's concern. It is bound to the fullness of being and human experience. The usual distinctions between private and public, religious and secular, collapse in the words of the prophet. The prophet becomes "political." It is within this voice that Gustavo Gutierrez demands a "prophetic *denunciation* of every dehumanizing situation, which is contrary to fellowship, justice, and liberty."[25] This is not to say that religion and the practice of faith are exempt from the prophet's concern. In the Hebrew Scriptures we hear the prophets Isaiah, Amos, and Hosea challenging not only the social practices of their times, but the religious practices of the people. Jesus is certainly not silent about the religious practices of the people, especially as practiced by the Pharisees. Martin Luther King Jr., in his classic text, "Letter from a Birmingham Jail" offers an excellent example. In the letter King, a fourth generation clergyman, writes of his deep disappointment with the church. ". . . I have wept over the laxity of the church. . . . Yes, I see the church as the body of Christ. But, oh! How we have blemished and scarred that body through social neglect and fear of being nonconformists."[26] This disappointment is founded not on hate for society and social practices, but on love. Dorothy Day has strong words of critique for the Church she loved: "I loved the Church for Christ made visible. Not for itself because it was so often a scandal to me. Romano Guardini said the Church is the Cross on which Christ was crucified; one could not separate Christ from His Cross, and one must live in a state of permanent dissatisfaction with the Church."[27] No aspect of life then is removed from the challenge. The prophet serves "as a conscience for his people in precisely those matters where conscience was needed,"[28] whether religious, economic, social, or political practices.

The prophet is a radical in the truest sense of the word. "Radical" denotes going to the roots or origins of a particular problem. His or her concern is not only with particular or isolated manifestations of evil, but with "systemic evils that pervade institutions and cultures, or that pervade the action and behavior of individual persons."[29] The prophet seeks to name the root evil that is expressed in particular evils. Because of this, the prophet is not merely interested in reforming social institutions so much as he or she is interested in challenging and transforming the very grounds on which these structures operate. The prophet challenges the ways social problems are commonly presented, thus, in effect, the prophet is calling people to see things at a different level. Cornel West offers a good example of this. In his book *Race Matters*, West addresses the current plight of African Americans. He reframes the way we would normally look at this issue as he disputes both the usual liberal "structuralist" and conservative "behaviorist" responses. These usual responses, he says, "have nearly suffocated the crucial debate that should be taking place about the prospects for black America." West concludes, "The most basic issue now facing black America [is] the nihilistic threat to its very existence."[30] He describes this threat as a "profound sense of psychological depression, personal worthlessness, and social despair so widespread in black America."[31]

The transformation called for by the prophet is more demanding than it might first appear. The prophet is not one who calls primarily for a particular policy or a specific law. What the prophet is about is challenging social structures as well as the persons who make up and support such structures. Indeed as Donal Dorr has suggested, the most significant structures in society might not be the cultural or economic systems, but rather "our patterns of thinking and feeling and valuing."[32] The prophet then is one who calls for radical social transformation and radical personal conversion. One of the things that makes a prophet or a prophecy so controversial is that few people stand outside his critique. Prophets insist that moral culpability goes beyond simply causing, supporting, or exploiting evil. The prophet challenges all "those who are in a position to avoid, eliminate, or limit social evils but who fail to do so out of laziness, fear . . . or indifference." They refuse to let persons "take refuge in the supposed impossibility of changing the world," or to let them "sidestep the effort and sacrifice required" in the name of some other goods.[33] The prophet recognizes very few excusing conditions for personal responsibility and social evil. As no aspect of life is removed from the prophet's concern, so no element of an individual's life is removed from prophetic concern. The range of the prophet's message is then both wide, the whole of human existence, and deep, the hearts and minds, indeed the soul, of individuals.

Jim Wallis captures this latter element in his discussion of Christian conversion. He writes,

> The way of Jesus and the prophets isn't just a welfare program; it calls for a change of heart, a revolution of the spirit, a transformation of our consciousness. It moves us beyond the familiar options of abandoning the poor, controlling the poor, or even "helping" the poor from places of isolation and comfort. Instead, it leads us to a new relationship with one another, a deep reconnection, a restoration of the shattered covenant.[34]

But how does one stir the conscience and indeed consciousness of another?

The second characteristic of the prophetic denunciation is the mode of discourse itself. The prophet realizes that true moral conversion begins with experience. The prophet pushes his or her audience to experience the evils described in the indictment. This is usually accomplished vicariously. That is, the prophet often takes the audience to visit the evil through narrative. Listeners can feel what it is like to be the victim of an oppressive, immoral system. More importantly, the prophet takes the audience to visit themselves. Using strong, passionate language filled with vibrant imagery, symbols and metaphor, the prophet stirs the conscience and moral imagination of listeners. As the prophet speaks, people are forced to look at themselves, their attitudes, and their roles in the social system. Do I support evil? Am I part of the conspiracy of silence? Have I become indifferent to the evil? While the prophet's words aim to evoke self-awareness, the language is never limited to introspection or mere reflection. Now is not the time for that; we do not have the luxury for this. People's lives are at stake. The prophet then seeks to evoke, in the words of Martin Luther King Jr., a sense of "the urgency of the now." The prophet demands a moral response from the listeners. In recent American history, the best example of prophetic discourse is King's 1963 "I Have a Dream" speech. Even today, watching the grainy black and white video, it is impossible to be untouched by his words. Hearing King's use of metaphor, the rightness of his message, the surety that exudes from his delivery, and the cadence of "I Have a Dream," awakens a sense of justice and hope in the viewer.[35]

I would not want to limit prophetic discourse to the spoken word. Sometimes what is left unsaid is as important as what is shouted from the mountain top. Moreover, we can include prophetic action as a subset of prophetic discourse. Prophetic action, that is, direct public activity such as picketing, boycotting, disrupting business as usual, or protesting can have several purposes. It may serve to educate people. It may serve to reveal to those in authority that there is a substantial and vocal voice of dissent. It may serve also to empower those who thought themselves powerless. For example, every year at the school where I teach, a student organization sponsors an event where students sleep outside in cardboard boxes. Their intent is to remind all who pass that the homeless are in our midst. Through their choosing to eat and sleep in these boxes, the students challenge the moral blindness of the campus community. The students know that their actions will not provide a single homeless person with a home that night. However, by making the issue public, they hope that others will volunteer at shelters, learn about the realities of homeless people, and eventually assist in solving this major social problem.

Here is another example: Land mines have become a major international issue. Many countries that were once at war (Angola and Bosnia to name two) are littered with land mines. After the fighting has stopped, who triggers these deadly devices? The answer is innocent people, often children. There have been protests around the world to ban the production and use of these indiscriminate killers. In my own city, there are people who meet every Tuesday morning at 7:30 outside the gates of a company that manufactures land mines. They protest and they pray. Sometimes one or two of them might purposefully venture onto the private property of the company and be arrested for trespassing. They then make the news and at their trials speak out about the evils of land mines in a very public forum. Their action is prophetic action.

Among the classical prophets, Isaiah went naked in public. Hosea kept and remained faithful to his prostitute wife. In the contemporary context, Jon Sobrino emphasizes the importance of Oscar Romero's "symbolic deeds." Sobrino describes the power that the martyred archbishop's actions conveyed. "Once and only once in the history of El Salvador, all of the churches of the archdiocese except the cathedral were closed on Sunday—so that all the faithful who wished could gather to celebrate one and the same Mass. Once and only once in the recent history of El Salvador, the Archbishop of San Salvador did not attend the solemn investiture of a President of the Republic."[36] In this case, Romero's action and his nonaction displayed a radical challenge to the status quo. Using provocative and passionate language or action, the prophet shocks his or her audience into recognition of the realities of our social order.

The third characteristic of the prophetic denunciation (the first being comprehensiveness of the indictment and the second the choice of language) is that the prophet emerges out of or is intimately and personally aware of the evil he or she preaches against. Put simply, the prophet has "been there." The prophet has personally experienced the evils he or she is condemning. Guiterrez writes, "Prophetic denunciation can be made validly and truly only from within the heart of the struggle for a more human world."[37] Sobrino says, "The prophet is a person on the street."[38] Prophets arise during a crisis. Their "authority" rests in their courage and authenticy in face of oppression. This process can happen in a number of ways. Rigoberta Menchu, the 1989 Noble Peace Prize winner, is the quintessential example of a person rising from within a community to lead others in the struggle for justice. Others, already in positions of authority, experience a conversion that compels them to speak. Archbishop Oscar Romero is an example of this. Still there are others, such as Dorothy Day, who make an "option for the poor" that intrinsically bind their lives to the lives of the poor. The prophet, after all, is not speaking for herself, but is rather speaking for God through speaking for the people. This link between the people and the prophet is crucial. The prophet arises within a tradition and its narratives, thus the ground for prophetic discourse rests on the practices, rituals, and stories of the community. Yet at the same time, the prophets are individuals. They hold the unique calling of bearing God's will. This burden, coupled with the prophet's constant critique of religious, political, and social institutions, makes the prophet something of an outsider in his or her own community.

Prophetic Hope

If the primary characteristic of the prophet is to denounce or indict, the other outstanding characteristic is to announce. The prophet is at once a sign of contradiction, a sign of hope, and in the final instance, a clarion of salvation. He calls us together and forward with the possibility, in the words of Gustavo Gutierrez, "of what is not yet, but will be . . . a forecast of a different order of things, a new society . . . of creative imagination which proposes the alternative values to those rejected."[39] The prophet paints a picture of a hopeful brighter future offering "an alluring vision of the future, of possibilities for life in the world in which the forms of strife and suffering we all experience are overcome."[40] When Martin Luther King Jr., for example, speaks of the time that "sons of former slaves and sons of former slave-owners will be able sit down together at the table of brotherhood,"[41] we can picture this, even though this vision is radically disparate from our lived experience. The utopian imagery of the prophet evokes our expectations and our aspirations.[42] People come to believe that what was once impossible is now a possibility. It can happen! There can be a different order in human relations. There can be a new society.[43] Thus Sobrino writes, "The prophet's ultimate word to the people was one of consolation and hope."[44] The vision, the utopian expectations of when, for example, people "shall beat their swords into plowshares and their spears into pruning hooks; nation shall not lift up sword against nation, neither shall they learn war any more" (Isaiah 2:4) offers the moral sustenance that empowers persons to work toward the transformation of social relations. This hope inspires confidence and breathes life into situations marked by despair. It is little wonder that the song, "We Shall Overcome" has become the anthem of civil rights movements across the globe. "Hope is," Jim Wallis comments, "the most feared reality of any oppressive system. More powerful than any other weapon, hope is the great enemy of those who would control history."[45]

True and False Prophets

A prophet then occupies a distinctive role in religion and public life. This calling or vocation can be distinguished from other recognized social positions such as ordained (or official) religious leaders, intellectuals, saints, and politicians, although all of these persons might engage prophetic language. The most common, or at least the most public, use of prophetic or prophetic-like discourse in the United States is in the political arena. Many politicians gain attention and favor through their denunciation of the status quo and through their use of imagery to suggest a utopian-like vision of a better America. Like the prophet, the politician often is able to hold together the seemingly disparate elements of the discourse through charisma or personality. Yet on several accounts the prophet, or the one who consistently uses prophetic discourse, is grossly out of step with the demands of the politician. Several biblical passages speak of false prophets, those prophets who, in the words of Bruce Vawter, were "deluded by their own prophetic devices, erring in judgment, confusing their own hopes and aspirations [or nationalist tendencies] with the authentic word of Yahweh."[46] The *Didache*, an early second century Christian text, counsels Christians to discern true prophets, namely, "those who behave like the Lord," from false prophets, who "trade on Christ."[47] The inquiry rests on the conduct and attitude of the prophet. Prophets who stay with the community more than two days are suspect as are those who ask for money. The text suggests a prima facie respect for prophets but offers this practical advice: "[E]very prophet who teaches the truth but fails to practice what he preaches is a false prophet."[48] The distinction between true and false prophets, though helpful, is not sufficient. To call one a "true" prophet does mean that the person is infallible. It does not mean that every time the prophet speaks, he or she speaks for God. For the biblical prophets, each "true prophetic word was in every case a distinct gift from God."[49] While a litmus test for true or false prophets or, more appropriately, true or false prophecy (outside of the conduct issue the *Didache* raises) would be impossible and perhaps inappropriate, there are several characteristics of prophets that put them at odds with the normal practice of politicians.

First, there is a consistent tension between the prophet and social institutions. Not only did classical prophets have very little "taste or talent for practical politics," they had an "instinctive dislike for the monarchy."[50] Prophets have a suspicion of the power structures whether religious, political or social. The weight of their vision simply cannot be captured in human institutions. Thus they cannot help seeing the shortcomings, failures and sins of human institutions. Moreover, as Gustafson notes, "prophets tend to be impatient with detailed analyses" necessary for good policy making. In the urgency of the now, prophets have little patience for gradualist step-by-step solutions and the patience it takes to develop policy. For the prophet, long-range studies, task forces, and sending it to a committee are essentially rearranging the deck chairs on the sinking Titanic.[51] The prophet often is silent on the actual procedures needed to create the new society. How do we get to the point that sons of former slaves and sons of former slave-owners can sit down at the table of brotherhood? The prophet's contributions lie more in vision and motivation than in practical solutions. The policymaker on the other hand must think in terms of the possible, of what is feasible.

While politics is "the art of compromise," prophetic language forces the question of "are you for or are you against?" There is no middle ground here. Because of this, prophets have a tendency to alienate large parts of the population who do not agree with them. The prophet is, after all, about radical critique, social transformation, and personal conversion. And even those who are sympathetic with the prophet and the prophet's cause can remain caught in the status quo, unable to move and fully support the prophet. King's critique of the white moderate is illustrative here. He writes, "I have almost reached the regrettable conclusion that the Negro's greatest stumbling block in the stride for freedom is not the . . . Ku Klux Klanner, but the white moderate who is more devoted to 'order' than to justice . . . Shallow understanding from people of good will is more frustrating than absolute misunderstanding from people of ill will."[52] Nevertheless, strong, affective language can change the way people think and feel about a certain issue. The prophet can motivate persons in a way that discourse on a particular public policy cannot. Because of this, prophetic or prophetic-like discourse can be a critical part of political campaigns. Yet there is a lingering issue separating the prophet from the politician. The politician must gain the public's favor. She must campaign and work to win public support. She must present and indeed boast of her competency and her virtues. The politician's personality is as much the message as is her platform.

On the other hand, the message of the prophet is of a decidedly different nature. As Dorothy Day wrote regarding the Catholic Worker movement, "Ours is indeed an unpopular front."[53] Prophets are not concerned with winning popularity contests. They do not judge their words and actions on a utilitarian-like calculus measuring social acceptance. As a conscience of a community, the prophet has the responsibility to tell the people what they might not want to hear. As was the case with Amos, many prophets are accused of treason or conspiracy (Amos 7:10). The F.B.I., for example, had some five hundred pages on file concerning the "subversive" activities of Dorothy Day and the Catholic Worker.[54] This is not to say that the gulf between prophet and politician is insurmountable. Andrew Young, Lech Walesa, and Vaclav Havel are examples of persons whose lives and abilities transcend these narrow categories.

A fundamental test for a true prophet is, "Whose side is he or she on?" Prophets can be from the "right" or the "left" on the political spectrum. They are united in a concern for the poor, powerless, and vulnerable in society.

Prophetic moral discourse, though laden with biblical roots and great motivational qualities, is not sufficient to cover the whole range of moral discourse, or indeed the range of needs of morally serious persons. The strengths of this form of moral discourse are obvious. Prophets move people to think, feel, and act in certain ways. The prophetic voice may indeed start the move through narrative, ethical, and policy forms of discourse. However, as Gustafson notes, there is a huge barrier "between prophetic voices and those that speak in more precise and rational modes of argumentation, and between the prophets and those whose callings require them to make choices within complex institutions and in difficult policy issues."[55] When all is said and done, many people would rather listen to the words of a prophet (especially one that does not directly challenge them) than read a philosophical treatment of justice. On the other hand, prophets alienate large numbers of people. They step on people's toes. Some believe they go too far to make their point. Most of the prophets I have known or heard about have spent time in jail, even in America, the land of free expression. We need prophets yet we need more than prophets. At times calm words ought to prevail and practical matters must be discussed.

The prophets I have mentioned above, King, Romero, Menchu, and Day have lived remarkable lives. King and Romero paid for their choices with their lives. However, we must be careful not to limit prophets to those who have been martyred or those who have lead extraordinary lives. While Isaiah was a prophet for most of his life, Amos was a prophet but for a short time. Hearing his call from God, Amos, the self-proclaimed "herdsman," left his fields in Judah and traveled north to Israel where he spoke out against the social practices (religious, legal, economic) of the people. When he was finished with his brief but bold critique, he went home. We know nothing more of him; so it is with many unnamed prophets today.

Where are the prophets today? So often it is hard to recognize or, rather, acknowledge contemporary prophets as they are in the middle of their struggle. I think this is the case because we, the public, do not know if they are right or wrong. It is very easy for me to cite King as a "truth-teller," a true prophet today. Most Americans would agree with me. If I were to have written this in 1963, this would be more controversial. Many Americans may have not held him in such esteem. Time has a way of helping us discern who is a true and who is a false prophet. Where are the prophets today? I see them in movements to protect children, to protect the innocent against the destructive might of militaries around the world, to defend people's freedom of conscience and religion, to protect the environment, and to challenge aspects of America's foreign policy that put expediency and profit above people.

If there is one thing clear about prophetic discourse, it is that not all of us are called to it as a vocation as were Isaiah or King. Yet to have moral integrity, all of us must step into that role on occasion. Try it. It may suit you.

CHAPTER THREE

The Kingdom of God Is at Hand

The Spirit of the Lord is upon me, because he has anointed
me to bring good news to the poor. He has sent me to
proclaim release to the captives and recovery of sight to the
blind, to let the oppressed go free, to proclaim the year of
the Lord's favor.

—Luke 4:18–19

JUSTICE: PARTICULAR AND UNIVERSAL

Our task in this book is twofold: to discuss the forms of moral discourse
and to discern how Christian faith informs a contemporary understanding
of justice. In the preceding chapters we explored the two primary forms
of moral discourse, narrative and prophetic. We also studied the Genesis
and Exodus narratives and the message of the eighth century prophets.
One way of understanding this twofold task is to say we are examining
both the form (the structure and procedure) and content (the substance)
of Christian morality. These texts provided us with a solid foundation
for both tasks. We have seen the significance of narrative as a primary
way people communicate moral ideas. We have also seen the power
and limitations of the prophetic form of discourse. Concerning the
content of justice, the Hebrew Scriptures proclaim that God is a God
who loves justice and is for justice. The "image of God" theme is a
statement commissioning persons to serve God and God's will, that is,
as God's stand-ins on earth. A primary responsibility of this is that we
are to be persons who love justice and persons who are for justice.
We are to be God's agents for justice. The Exodus event and the words
of the prophets provide us with some directives of what loving justice
and being for justice entail. There is a clear indication in these texts
of God's concern for the poor, the oppressed, and the powerless
in society.

This chapter will address the question of particularity (is justice
selective? does it only pertain to particular people?) and universality

(does justice involve all? can the ideas be generalized beyond the Christian community?) in these texts. It will then explore the life, teachings, and death of Jesus.

The Hourglass Effect

The biblical notion of justice holds together insights that are seemingly contradictory. According to the prophets, officials ought to be impartial in the administration of legal justice. They must hear the legitimate claims of all persons. In the social order, which includes the law, the people must be partisan. They must defend the poor and powerless. This seems to be a logical contradiction. Justice here entails mutually exclusive ends, objectivity on one hand and partiality on the other. This contradiction personifies a deeper contradiction in the Hebrew Bible, namely, the justice of God. In many places in the Hebrew Scriptures, God is described as being just and loving justice, God of all. Yet this God also has favorites. This contradiction, this "scandal of particularity" poses theoretical problems as we develop a conception of justice.

After reviewing the Creation and Exodus narratives as well as the message of the prophets, we can see the nature of this contradiction and perhaps the resolution of this contradiction. When we read these three sources together, we see what might be called an "hourglass" effect. These three stories read back-to-back display a movement between the universality and the particularity of the justice of God. An hourglass is wide at the top, narrow in the middle and wide at the bottom. The Creation stories, the Exodus event, and the words of the prophets mirror an hourglass. Moshe Weinfeld writes that in the Hebrew Scriptures, God established justice in these three paradigmatic situations, all of which are associated with God's kingship. The first is the creation of the world. The Creation stories are universalistic in intent and scope. The subject after all is the creation of the cosmos. The particular humans created symbolize the creation of all humanity. All of us are created in the image of God. All are to be responsible representatives of God on earth. Justice at creation, Weinfeld states, "refers to the imposition of equality, order and harmony upon the cosmos and the elimination of the forces of destruction and chaos."[1] The implications are universal, the bottom of the hourglass.

The second establishment of justice by God is the Exodus event. This event includes both the liberation of people from slavery and the giving of the law. The Exodus story and the covenant between God and the Israelites celebrate particularity—God's special relationship, God's covenant with the Israelites. One can realistically imagine that there were many people or nations around the globe who lived under an oppressive regime at the time of the Exodus. The universal God, at least as is told in the Bible, saved only the Israelites. There were many, many other peoples with whom God could have formed covenants, but God chose the Israelites. As we read in the Book of Amos, "You only have I known of all the families of the earth" (Am 3:2). God may very well have been saving and making covenants with other peoples, but the Christian tradition, based as it is on the Jewish tradition, knows this God primarily through God's relation to the Jews. They are our spiritual ancestors. In the Exodus, states Weinfeld, "we find both social equality and political freedom."[2] The hourglass is narrow; the concern is particular.

The Exodus, the very particular story of God's saving action, becomes the universal story of God's saving activity. Analogical reasoning holds that the initial step in knowing the universal God is not through abstract theories or generalizations but through particular experiences or relationships. One, for example, does not really know the meaning of the term "love" through textbook definitions or philosophical treatises. One comes to know and understand love through loving, being loved, and seeing other people love each other. A person cannot really love everyone if he or she has never loved anyone. It is from particulars, namely experiences and relationships, that persons can make more general and abstract statements about the nature and reality of love. "The movement to the universal occurs only in the embrace of the particular."[3] William Spohn argues that particulars, not universals, are the basis of ethics. "Moral concepts derive from patterns in particular experiences; moral reflection moves analogically from paradigmatic cases to more problematic ones that contain novel elements."[4] The biblical narratives in their particularities, the Exodus, the chosen people, communicate understanding about the nature of the universal God.

Gustavo Gutierrez offers a compelling and challenging commentary on the question of the universal God and particular relationships. His analogical reasoning expands the people of Israel to humanity and the poor and powerless in Israel to the oppressed everywhere. Thus the tension for Gutierrez is between the universal God who loves all of creation and the God who has a unique concern for the poor and oppressed. How does Gutierrez resolve this philosophical quandary?

He writes, "I insisted that the great challenge was to maintain both the universality of God's love and God's predilection for those on the lowest rung of the ladder of history. To focus exclusively on the one or the other is to mutilate the Christian message. Therefore every attempt at such an exclusive emphasis must be rejected."[5] The tension here is like the tension evident in other doctrines of the Christian faith that seek to unify logically conflicting claims. For example, God is both transcendent and God is immanent. Jesus is both fully human and fully divine. There are three people in the one God. A key theme here (logically problematic and linguistically ironic), both for Gutierrez and the biblical prophets, is that to know the universal and all-powerful God, one must know particular poor and powerless people.

It is important to note that particularity is not the only theme in the Hebrew Scriptures. Like an hourglass, the narratives become universal again. The third work of justice by God is the future time of universal redemption announced in the Psalms and addressed by the prophets. At this time the messiah-king will rule, judge, and arbitrate among the nations (Is 2:4, 11:4). In this time salvation and liberation will not only be within nations, it will be between nations. This is like the top of the hourglass; the concern is broad and universal. Indications of what universal salvation will be like are evident in the words of the prophets. The universality of the prophets comes in both explicit and implicit forms. As noted above, Amos' proclamation to the Israelites is prefaced by explicit indictments of seven surrounding peoples, six who are not covenant partners with God. It is not inappropriate to ask Amos on what grounds he could condemn these people given that they organized their societies on different laws than the Israelites. These people, after all, did not acknowledge Israel's God. Amos indicts these nations on the charge of war crimes, namely the slaughter of citizens, genocide, treaty violations and the desecration of the dead.[6] These crimes are an affront to the universal God. The presupposition here is that there is some basic or foundational morality beyond the covenant that God recognizes and indeed authorizes. The implication of the indictments offered by Amos is that the nations themselves must acknowledge their crimes.

The issue of particularity and universality must also be addressed on the interpretative level. While the prophets are steeped in their own culture and time and their message is directed to their own historical moment, contemporary reflection on their sense of justice indicates a universality in their message. A good society by its nature tries to combine the two faces of justice evident in the words of the prophets. It promotes the just claims of all in its legal system. It does not exclude persons from participating because they are poor nor does it give preference to some because they are rich. Arbiters, judges, and officials must not take bribes. This objectivity and impartiality are cornerstones of a moral society. On the other hand, the community must passionately protect the interests and needs of the least powerful persons in society. They must side with the poor in the face of aggressive tendencies of the rich. This partiality is another cornerstone of a moral society.

Justice Constituted by Compassion

There is a final characteristic of justice in the Hebrew Bible. Jon Levenson, following Weinfeld, notes that the ancient Hebrew texts about justice are often translated "to do justice and righteousness." This translation can lead readers to think primarily in terms of the legal system and justice in the courts. Levenson states that the ancient Hebrew text denotes a meaning beyond the courtroom. In fact, the Hebrew Bible often links justice and compassion. He cites Zechariah 7:9–10 as an example. "Thus said the LORD of Hosts: Execute true justice; deal loyally and compassionately with one another. Do not defraud the widow, the orphan, the stranger, and the poor; and do not plot evil against one another." Levenson concludes,

> It would be a mistake to see in these words a call to justice *tempered* by compassion, or to a compassion that *goes beyond* justice. . . . Rather, justice here is *constituted by* compassion, by special solicitude for the powerless and disadvantaged, a determination that they not be victimized. That determination is not peculiar to courts of law. The Hebrew Bible expects it of everyone.[7]

Justice is constituted by compassion. "Constituted" here means that it is an elemental and necessary part of justice. "Compassion" denotes the ability to "step inside the shoes of another," to feel what another is feeling, to sense when and what another is suffering. The words in Exodus illustrate how compassion is an elemental and necessary part of justice, "Out of the slavery their cry for help rose to God. God heard their groaning" (Ex 2:23–24). Analogically speaking, "Out of oppression their cry to help rose to God. God heard their groaning and God's representatives responded."

COMPASSION AND KINGDOM

In the person of Jesus of Nazareth the two primary forms of moral discourse, prophetic and narrative, are united. Jesus was an excellent storyteller. He knew the power of a good story. Several of his parables, the Good Samaritan and the Prodigal Son for example, are classic stories. The Christian tradition, however, does not simply pass on these ancient stories. In an ironic twist, the storyteller becomes the subject of the story. The story of Jesus, his life, teachings, actions, death and resurrection, is the foundation of the Christian life. It is this narrative, not dogma nor laws nor philosophy, that is the crucial ground of the Christian experience. Indeed dogma or law must be rooted in the narrative to have a definitive claim on the Christian conscience.

Jesus was more than a storyteller. His parables are but one element of his ministry. Jesus was also a prophet in line with the tradition of the eighth century prophets. His words, like Amos and Isaiah, ring out with characteristic denouncement and announcement (see for example, Luke 6:20–26). Unlike Amos and other prophets in the Hebrew Bible, however, Jesus is not primarily a prophet of doom and destruction. For Jesus the first word is the good news and hope because, as he proclaimed, "the Kingdom of God is at hand" (Mt 4:17). Luke, for example, records Jesus' first public words as, "The Spirit of the Lord is upon me, because he has anointed me to bring good news to the poor" (Luke 4:18). Jesus states that the purpose for which he was sent was to proclaim this good news of the kingdom of God (Luke 4:42). The narratives, the parables, are in service of this proclamation.

Jesus, however, was more than just storyteller, prophet, and teacher. That is to say, he was not simply a speaker, a person of words. He was a doer, an activist. In a verse that summarizes Jesus' work, Luke writes, "When the crowds found out [where Jesus was] . . . they followed him; and he welcomed them, and spoke to them about the kingdom of God, and he healed those who needed to be cured" (Luke 9:11). There are two parallel aspects of Jesus' public ministry. He cared for people. He proclaimed the Kingdom of God. The remaining sections of this chapter will explore these parallel aspects.

He Healed Those Who Needed to Be Cured

One of the first things my students note when reading a Gospel is the number of miracles Jesus performed. When we read a Gospel in a class on Christian morality, they often have to look hard to find Jesus's moral teaching. His "teachings" here are, of course, expressed through his actions. After some reflection, students can see some characteristics of these miracle stories and how they are an essential element of Jesus' moral teachings. Most of Jesus' miracles deal with the physical well-being of people. Jesus stands against evil and suffering in its many forms and affirms personal worth through establishing health and human well-being. What does Jesus do? He heals people. He feeds people. He casts out the demons who limit their ability to choose and to act. In the Gospel of Luke, for example, it is impossible to count the number of people Jesus healed. There are over a dozen occasions where Luke mentions that Jesus healed people (See for example Luke 4:38; 4:40; 5:13; 5:24; 6:19; 7:10; 7:15; 7:21; 8:36; 8:46; 8:50; 13:13; 14:4). Luke is not alone; all four of the Gospels proclaim Jesus' active commitment to the well-being of others. In many of the healing stories, Jesus reaches out and touches the person being healed. Usually he lays his hands on the person. However, Luke records a case where the opposite is true. A woman touches Jesus' clothes and is healed (Luke 8:43–48). It is noteworthy that in the majority of healing narratives, Jesus cures individuals, not groups of people. Moreover, it is never said that Jesus eradicates a disease. He cures lepers but does not rid the earth of leprosy. He feeds the thousands on the hill but does not alleviate world hunger. Jesus is touched by individuals and he touches individuals. The healings and other miracles are prophetic actions signaling the presence of the kingdom and a start of a new era in human history.

Jesus' actions serve to ground and justify his teachings. Consider one of the most quoted parables of Jesus, the Good Samaritan, in the longer narrative about the Double Love Command. Luke begins this narrative with a lawyer confronting Jesus. The lawyer pushes Jesus on a hard theological question. He asks Jesus what he must do to gain eternal life. Jesus responds to the lawyer's question with another question. He returns with a confrontation question himself testing the man's knowledge of Scripture. Jesus asks the man what the Scripture says about eternal life. The lawyer answers in what is now referred to as the "Double Love Command." (In Matthew's and Mark's Gospels Jesus is the one who states the double love command. See Mt 22:36–40 and Mk 12:29–31.) "You shall love the Lord your God with all your heart, and with all your soul, and with all your strength, and with all your mind; and your neighbor as yourself" (Luke 10:27). Jesus affirms the lawyer and his answer, but the lawyer pursues the line of questioning.

He asks Jesus, "And who is my neighbor?" He wanted a definition. Jesus replies not with a definition or a legal code, but with the story of the Good Samaritan.

This is a compelling story that readily invites the hearer into its plot. Hearers can identify and feel the feelings of all the characters; the story evokes compassion. We all can identify with the man who was in need yet who was ignored and passed by. How many times have you been hurt, emotionally or physically, and looked for help, only to be ignored by others? We all have had situations where we did not stop to help another in need. Hopefully we can all recall times when we did come to the aid of another, and we all have at sometime or another been helped when hurt.

Martin Luther King Jr. gives us an insightful commentary on this story. He begins describing his own journey with his wife down the road from Jerusalem to Jericho, the setting for Jesus' narrative.

> The Jericho Road was a dangerous road. . . . As we traveled slowly down that meandering, mountainous road, I said to my wife, "I can now understand why Jesus chose this road as the setting for his parable." Jerusalem is some two thousand feet above and Jericho one thousand feet below sea level. The descent is made in less than twenty miles. Many sudden curves provide likely places for ambushing and expose the traveler to unforeseen attacks. Long ago the road was known as the Bloody Pass. So it is possible that the priest and the Levite were afraid that if they stopped, they too would be beaten. Perhaps the robbers were still nearby. Or maybe the wounded man on the ground was a faker, who wished to draw passing travelers to his side for quick and easy seizure.[8]

King highlights the risks involved in "putting yourself in the shoes" of the beaten man. His personal narrative suggests that stopping to help a stranger along the road to Jericho while Jesus lived was as risky as stopping to help a stranger along any road in our time.

There are other nuances of the story, stories within the story, that make the Good Samaritan a classic narrative. Jesus tells us that the priest and Levite (an associate of the priest) saw the wounded man and crossed over to the other side of the road. The people we would expect to help did nothing. King speculates on their "reason" for not helping. Maybe they were afraid. Others have suggested a different reasoning.

Perhaps the priest and Levite were on their way to a religious service. If they were and they came in contact with the victim's blood, they would be "impure." They would be unable to perform the ritual. If this was the case, Jesus was no doubt making a point on what really mattered. The well-being of people was more important than the principles associated with religious ritual. Like the message of the eighth century prophets, morality is more important than ritual.

There is a "great reversal" in this story. The people who could be counted on to lead a faithful life, the priest and Levite, were moral and religious failures, but that the moral hero was a Samaritan. For Jesus' audience the fact that the hero is not one of them (the hero is not a Christian either! There is no record of the Good Samaritan making any profession of faith!), but a member of a despised group, was shocking. A Samaritan, a member of a disliked race of people, stopped and attended to this man's needs. Not only did this man help the beaten man, he put him on his horse (or donkey), brought him to an inn, and gave the innkeeper enough money to keep the man while he recovered!

As Jesus finishes the story, he asks the lawyer another question, "Which of these three, do you think was a neighbor to the man who fell into the hands of the robbers?" The lawyer answers abstractly, perhaps not wanting to admit that the Samaritan was the hero. He says, "The one who showed him mercy." Irony and surprise run through the story Jesus tells as well as the story Luke tells about Jesus telling the story. The lawyer's initial question suggests that some people are our neighbors and others are not. "Jesus' story replies that there is no one who is not my neighbor."[9]

From a question about eternal life, we hear about loving God and loving neighbor. This love is illustrated by the concrete act of a stranger moved by compassion for a person in need. The narrative and the incident with the lawyer conclude with Jesus saying, "Go and do likewise." Is this about justice?

The priest and the Levite foolishly thought they were doing justice to God, giving God what was due, namely "purity" at the time of ritual. The narrative proclaims an important message, however, that one cannot fulfill one's responsibilities to God unless one fulfills one's responsibilities to others. The link between serving others and serving God is as clear in this narrative as it is in the words of the prophets. The Samaritan did act justly toward the victim. The victim was due something from the Samaritan, as well as from the priest and Levite. He was due minimum care. The Samaritan did much more than was required by justice. His compassion moved him from justice to a self-sacrificing care for the other.

Narratives of Care

"Christians" by definition are followers of Jesus Christ. Thus Christian morality and Christian conceptions of justice begin with the faith statement that Jesus is the Christ, the Son of God. As we saw in the first chapter of this book, in the New Testament, Jesus is described as the "image of God." This not only tells us something about Jesus, it tells us something about who we are to be and what we ought to do. If we are to be God's responsible representatives, then we are to be like Jesus. The narrative of Jesus' life becomes an imperative for his followers. There is an irony here. We are to be of service to others, especially those in need, those who are hurt, and those who are powerless, if we are to follow Jesus, but it is also through this service that we come to know Jesus.

The key to understanding the Christian moral life is that one's relation to God is only as good as one's relations to one's neighbor. This insight is illustrated, often quietly, all the time. I would like to offer two examples, one from literature and the other a story of a contemporary person, that further illustrates the nature of compassion that constitutes the biblical notion of justice.

The example from literature is from Shusaku Endo's work *Deep River*. In this wonderful novel, Endo introduces his readers to several contemporary Japanese characters looking for meaning in their lives. One of the central characters of the book, Kiguchi, reflects on a terrible and horrifying time in his life. When he was a soldier in the Japanese army during World War II, he and many other Japanese soldiers trudged through Burma on what can only be called a "walk through hell." Many soldiers died of starvation and exhaustion. Many killed themselves along the way because they could no longer endure the pain. Kiguchi, however, survived, but not on his own accord. He owed his life to his companion Tsukada who helped him through that evil time. Once when both were nearly dead from the march and starvation, Tsukada came across a dead cow and was somewhat energized by eating its meat. Kiguchi was too sick to eat but Tsukada was able to carry him to safety.

Many years later, in a subway station, Kiguchi and Tsukada meet. Kiguchi is a successful businessman while Tsukada, troubled by drinking problems, is unable to hold a job. His drinking ultimately leads to serious medical problems and to his deathbed. Tsukada cannot seem to control his need for drink; and soon we learn why. He must blot out the memory of an evil act he performed. The memory of this act is killing him vicariously though his need to drink. This evil, this unforgivable act, was that during the march though Burma, it was not a dead cow that he happened upon, but a dead comrade. He did not offer Kiguchi beef but human flesh. Indeed the flesh was of a fallen man in his military company. After the war, Tsukada is haunted by this act, indeed he can hardly face himself after he met the widow and son of this man.

While sick in the hospital, Tsukada meets Gaston. Gaston is a foreigner, a visitor to Japan, volunteering at the hospital where Tsukada is a patient. Gaston uses his volunteer time not only to serve patients but also to learn Japanese. He ends up playing a critical role in Tsukada's liberation and redemption. In a moving incident Gaston cares for Tsukada as Tsukada vomits and profusely bleeds. Tsukada then confesses his crime to Gaston. "Can your God forgive this?" he asks Gaston. The reader, of course, realizes that Tsukada means "Can God forgive me?" Gaston replies to his question with a story of the plane crash in the Andes Mountains a few years back where the people survived for seventy-two days by eating the flesh of those who died in the crash. The families of the victims held nothing against the survivors. The narrative continues from this point:

> Gaston exhausted every word he knew in Japanese to comfort Tsukada. He came to Tsukada's room every day after that and held the dying man's hands between his own palms, talked to him and encouraged him. Kiguchi could not tell whether such comfort eased Tsukada's pain. But the figure of Gaston kneeling beside the bed looked like a bent nail, and the bent nail struggled to become one with the contortions of Tsukada's mind, and to suffer along with Tsukada.
>
> Two days later, Tsukada died. His face was more at peace than anyone had imagined it could be, but a look of peace always comes at last to the dying. "He looks like he's sleeping," Tsukada's wife mumbled, but Kiguchi couldn't help but feel that his peaceful death-mask had been made possible because Gaston had soaked up all the anguish in Tsukada's heart.[10]

Gaston "soaked up all the anguish in Tsukada's heart" with his listening, his words, and his compassion that lead Tsukada to a place of liberation. Gaston, through a compassion moved to justice, lived his

responsibilities to the fullest extent. This meant liberation not domination, hope not despair, and emotional well-being not sickness. Gaston
knew that Tsukada was due something, that he deserved particular
treatment.

The second example of this compassion to justice is from a narrative
by Robert Inchausti about Mother Teresa. Inchausti writes:

> A few years ago I saw Mother Teresa on television. It was just
> after the Beirut bombing by Israel in which so many civilians were
> killed. Mother Teresa was helping place two wounded little girls
> into an ambulance when she was accosted by several reporters.
> One of them asked her if she thought her relief efforts were
> successful given the fact that there were a hundred other children
> in another bombed-out hospital that she wasn't getting any aid
> to. She replied, "Don't you think it is a good thing to help these
> little ones?" The reporter did not flinch but simply asked his
> question again: "The other hospital has many wounded children
> too. Can you call your efforts successful if you leave them unat-
> tended?" Mother Teresa ignored his repeated question and, with
> an obstinacy worthy of an American politician, answered her own:
> "I think it is a good thing to help these children." She did not say this
> with scorn, or anger, or even exasperation, but with immovable
> determination.
>
> And then as her shoulder sank beneath the weight of the
> stretcher, she gave the reporter a glance that asked, "Why don't
> you help me lift these children into the ambulance; that is some-
> thing you can do." It was one of those rare moments . . . when
> the confusions of the world were defeated, if only for a moment,
> by a practical act of love. Mother Teresa's love not only for the
> children but for the reporter in his own moral pain. And I like
> to think that somewhere in that reporter's soul a hope was sparked,
> if only for a second, that there was something he could do.[11]

Mother Teresa incarnated Jesus' love because she saw Jesus incarnated in other people, especially in the broken bodies of the poor. Her
compassion, no simple sentiment, was the determinative guide for her
of personal responsibility for others. We Americans cannot imagine the
poverty, sickness, and awful living conditions that the people whom
she ministered to live and die in. Both narratives witness compassion.
Gaston and Mother Teresa, like the Good Samaritan, felt the experiences

of the other. Inchausti's point is that Mother Teresa also knew the "pain" of all those who stand by and watch others suffer.

The Particular and the Universal

There are lingering problems, however, in both of these narratives. The reporter's question, with all of its cold and calculating trappings, does contain an element of truth. What about those other children? Or, more profoundly, why are those children there? Why the bombing? Why the war? Why do the conditions exist that forced these children into this situation? People, after all, have caused this suffering. Recall the context in which Tsukada found himself. The war was not his choice. He was responding, as best he could, to the horrible conditions of war forced on him through the decisions and actions of others. What about the bigger picture? We must, like Jesus himself and Mother Teresa in Inchausti's story and Gaston in *Deep River*, serve others from compassion that moves justice. But there is more.

Let us return for a moment to the Double Love Command. For Luke, the parable of the Good Samaritan is not the conclusion to the discourse about the Double Love Command. Immediately following the parable we read that Jesus goes to the house of two sisters, Mary and Martha. Mary is said to have "sat at the Lord's feet and listened to what he was saying" (Luke 10:39), while Martha worked in the house. Martha complains to Jesus about Mary because she is not helping her. Jesus replies that Martha is too distracted and that Mary has chosen the right thing to do. In our day, this story might get filed in that category of "uninteresting." However for Jesus' audience, there again was an important shock and reversal in this story. Jesus is acting against the dominant cultural norms of his day, again, a prophetic action. He is in a house, alone with women not his relatives.[12] This is not appropriate. Moreover, he is teaching one of them! As Verhey states, "No self-respecting rabbi could or would endure teaching a woman."[13] Luke's phrasing of the incident is bold. He says that Mary was sitting at the feet of Jesus. This language describes a master-disciple relationship. Jesus accepted Mary as one of his disciples.[14] It is the better way, the way of discipleship that she chooses and her sister does not. Mary was paying attention to Jesus and Martha was not and Jesus was paying attention to Mary.

Jesus' act of teaching Mary, in her home, was a single act of broad significance. Luke's description of this act not only expresses Jesus' love and friendship for Mary but also forces the listeners of the story to wonder about their perception of what is right and what is wrong. This particular act pushes general questions of human relationships. In it the question of the bigger picture is addressed through a simple act. In Jesus, the particular and the universal are united.

He Spoke to Them about the Kingdom of God

The main theme in the teachings of Jesus is the Kingdom of God. Indeed it can be argued that Jesus' actions, including his healings, were in service of the kingdom. However, as Verhey has written, what Jesus meant by the Kingdom of God "has been a matter of considerable dispute."[15] There are several reasons why the issue is controversial. They include the fact that contemporary frameworks for thinking about political structures are radically different from those of the time of Jesus; a kingdom can refer to place and/or action; and Jesus often used paradoxical language to describe the kingdom.

At first glance, we moderns have to overcome a huge cultural gap in understanding Jesus. The notion of "kingdom" seems quaint and archaic to our ears. I have never lived in a kingdom nor have I experienced living under a king. I have been raised in a culture that had its origins in a revolution against a king and the whole notion of a kingdom. In my heart, reared on freedom and democracy, I hold the notion of kingship with some disdain. However, for the people in Jesus' time, the notions of kingship, lordship, dominion were central concepts of social life.[16] The Israelites lived in a kingdom; but it was not their own kingdom. They lived in Caesar's kingdom, the Roman Empire. They were a nation under the power of the sword and the military rule of another nation. This had not always been the case. The Israelites once were a kingdom unto themselves. Indeed many people during Jesus' time looked forward to the day when they would be a nation once again. All this talk of authoritarianism is troublesome to modern sensibilities. It contradicts fundamental elements of our notion of justice, especially as justice is equated with political freedoms and political equality.[17] For Jesus' audience, however, quite the opposite was true. When Jesus used the word "kingdom," his people had strong mental images of three historical snapshots: what they were, what they are, and what they hoped to be.

A kingdom is a political, social, and cultural reality and the king is the determining factor in the formation of the meaning for this reality. The notion of a "kingdom," however, does not only refer to a geographical territory. It also denotes a form of governance, a reign of a king. Indeed some biblical translations speak of the "Reign of God" rather than the "Kingdom of God." This is the sense of kingdom that Jesus proclaimed. The Kingdom of God is not limited to or located in a specific territory.

When Jesus speaks directly about the kingdom he uses paradoxical language. The kingdom is "already, but not yet"; it is "in time" but "outside of time"; it is a gift from God that requires human action; it is characterized by a reversal of common expectations and standards. The first paradoxical element in Jesus' teaching on the kingdom is that it is "already but not yet." The kingdom has begun with the ministry of Jesus, but it will not be fulfilled in his lifetime, our lifetime, indeed in human history. In the ordinary understanding of the term "kingdom," there is no ambiguity. You are either in a kingdom or you are not. The answer to the question, "Is God's kingdom here?" is, "Yes and no." It is but it is not. The kingdom, says Jesus, is a present reality (see Luke 11:20) and a future reality (see Luke 22:30).

The questions "when?" and "where?" are important. Some Christians have tended to highlight the future "not yet" and exclude the present "already." They then define the Kingdom of God as heaven, the afterlife. This could lead to an overspiritualization of faith that is unwarranted by the biblical texts and has little to do with the moral demands of Jesus. Think of the most famous Christian prayer, the Lord's Prayer, found in Luke 11:2–4 and Matthew 6:9–15. When Christians pray, "Your kingdom come. Your will be done, on earth as it is in heaven," they are not praying to go somewhere, they are praying for a certain type of relationship to exist among people and within creation.[18] The Kingdom of God reveals a truth about human living and human good. It is, in a sense, a vision of how things ought to be. Gustavo Gutierrez argues that Jesus' teaching on the kingdom reveals to persons, "the aspiration for a just society and leads [people] to discover unsuspected dimensions and unexplored paths. The kingdom is realized in a society of fellowship and justice; and, in turn, this realization opens up the promise and hope of complete communion of all persons with God. The political is grafted into the eternal."[19]

Others, at the opposite end of interpretation, have been accused of highlighting the "already" and ignoring the "not yet."[20] This can lead to simplistic identification of the coming of the kingdom with specific public positions. What is unclear for us is clear for Jesus, the Kingdom of God is present but not yet fulfilled; it is here in human time and human history, but it is beyond human time and human history. The appropriate response of Christians is to respect both aspects of the kingdom and to live in the tension between the vision of the fullness of the kingdom and its partial but concrete actualization in our lives.[21]

A third paradoxical element in Jesus' teaching on the kingdom is that the kingdom is a gift of God freely given, yet it also demands human activity. The first part of this paradox suggests two beliefs. The first is that God is king, and if God is king then all human kingships, lordships, and dominion are relativized. No form of human authority can be absolute and command absolute obedience. If God is king then all forms of human domination are suspect, whether in the political sphere, business life, or the family. All forms of human authority must be examined from the point of view of Jesus' teachings. Living in the tension between the "already and not yet" demands that Christians keep a careful eye on all forms of human control over other humans. The second point is that God's action and only God's action will bring about the kingdom. The kingdom is not dependent on human activity. Scripture scholar Benedict Viviano writes that the kingdom represents "the future, final salvation of all humanity, socially, politically, and spiritually through an exercise of the sovereignty of God, establishing justice and peace on earth as well as in heaven."[22] Clearly only God can bring this about.

One might conclude from these statements that an appropriate response of Christians then is to do nothing except keep an attentive eye out for God's work in history. Even a cursory reading of the New Testament, however, would not allow for this kind of response. Jesus was not a philosopher and his followers were not contemplatives. He was an activist, a person concerned about other people. His healings, exorcisms, and feedings were signs, perhaps even sacraments, of the kingdom. Christians, who by definition are followers of Jesus, are to keep up his work. We are to "go and do likewise."

Indeed this is the ethic of Jesus: We are to respond to God's present action, the "already," in our lives.[23] The kingdom is then realized every day, indeed every moment of every day when people are like Jesus to other people, like Mother Teresa or Gaston. In the Gospel of Matthew, Jesus talks about the end of time and the fulfillment of the kingdom. He describes the criterion on how he will divide the nations: "I was hungry and you gave me food, I was thirsty and you gave me something to drink; I was a stranger and you welcomed me, I was naked and you gave me clothing; I was sick and you took care of me, I was in prison and you visited me" (Mt 25:35–36). The people are surprised. They wonder, "When did we do this?" and Jesus replies, "I tell you, whenever you did this for one of the least of these who are members of my family, you did it for me" (Mt 25:40).

The fourth paradoxical element of Jesus' teaching of the Kingdom of God can be found in the words Jesus uses to talk about it. Jesus often uses figures of speech to describe the kingdom. Figures of speech such as hyperbole and metaphor prod us, shock us, and encourage us to look at things differently.[24] Jesus challenges his listeners to step out of their usual expectations and discover what the Kingdom of God is like. Verhey describes Jesus' teaching on the kingdom as a "great reversal of the present age."[25] The parables, sayings, and indeed the actions of Jesus are often characterized as a reversal of what people expect. In contrast to the expected rule of the Messiah, for example, there are no nationalistic visions of a new earthly power in Jesus' teaching of the kingdom. His emphasis is not on the powerful nor is it on the might of the military. His emphasis is on the poor and sick, the hungry and sorrowful. The coming of the kingdom will cause a "great reversal" of values. Our response to God's action is then not to further it by force or intimidation or threat. Force used in the name of the kingdom of people, not in the name of the Kingdom of God. It can never be used by people in the name of the Kingdom of God. The Kingdom of God, while something people enter into, also enters into people. Yet such openness is different from what common wisdom would suggest. Verhey writes, "The present order, including its conventional rule of prestige and protocol, pomp and privilege, is called into question by Jesus' announcement of the coming kingdom. The expectation of God's rule is condensed into axioms like 'many that are first will be last, and the last first' and 'whoever exalts himself will be humbled and whoever humbles himself will be exalted.'"[26]

The Kingdom of God is Jesus' annunciation, his alluring vision. It is not a utopian vision if "utopian" is meant to mean an impossible and improbable dream. The kingdom is characterized by certain types of relationships among people. As Jesus talks, it will be a universal experience. As we live, it is partially actualized in particular contexts. Here the "not yet" comes into being. The kingdom also pushes us to look for the Reign of God even in the reign of violence and despair. We need to encourage the development of the conditions for the possibility of persons seeing and experiencing God's kingdom. In the famous words of Peter Maurin, "We need to make the kind of society where it is easier for people to be good."[27]

In the person of Jesus, the two primary forms of moral discourse are united. His narratives, especially his parables, have had an enduring effect on the imagination of his followers. They continue to challenge listeners to think about what sort of persons they ought to be. Moreover, Jesus' life, teachings, death and resurrection have become *the* narrative for Christian identity. Jesus was also a prophet in line with the classical prophets. His style of moral leadership propels Christians to endorse prophetic discourse. His proclamation of the kingdom and indeed his very life announced a new era in human history. This new era, however, offers interpretive problems for the contemporary Christian. What are we to make of this?

CHAPTER FOUR

The Bible and Ethical Theory

And how is it that we hear, each of us, in our own native
language?

—Acts 2:8

JESUS, COMMUNITY, AND THE WORLD

Last summer I was teaching a class that explored the writings of several
social activists. It was a graduate class in the Department of Education
so my students were reflective adults active in the teaching field for
years. We started the semester reading *The Long Loneliness*, Dorothy
Day's autobiography. The book describes the variety of loves in Day's
life, especially her love for the poor. Day narrates the beginnings of
the Catholic Worker community and its effort to publicly live the works
of mercy, namely, "to feed the hungry; to give drink to the thirsty; to
clothe the naked; to harbor the harborless; to ransom the captive; to
visit the sick; to bury the dead."[1] Among other things, Day describes
the times she protested war, the times she spent in jail, the many times
she walked the picket lines with striking workers, and the houses of
hospitality she (and the movement) started around the country.

During the second or third class, a student reflected on her own
upbringing in relation to Day's writing. She said growing up Catholic
she was very familiar with what Day stood for. She knew the philosophy
that grounded Day's work. Another student, who happened to be a
good friend of the first, stated that the material was quite foreign to
her. She had grown up in a Lutheran household in a small town. The
moral demand in her youth, she said, was to take care of our own.
This conversation was interesting for me because it mirrored a discussion
current in Christian morality. The issue can be framed this way: What
is the appropriate form that Christian life should take? Should Christians
work diligently to change the world or should Christians work diligently
to form and nurture Christian communities? The first option holds that

the primary social ethic of the church is to defend the nameless needy and oppressed people. The second holds that "the first social task of the church is to be the church."[2]

Richard Hays defends the latter position. He argues that the New Testament calls us to "form communities that will embody the truth of the Word, demonstrating metaphorically the power of God's grace in our midst."[3] His reading of the Sermon on the Mount suggests what a Christian community might look like. Hays writes, "In sum, the kingdom of God as figured forth in Matthew 5 is full of surprises. Matthew offers a vision of a radical countercultural community of discipleship characterized by a 'higher righteousness'—a community free of anger, lust, falsehood, and violence. The transcendence of violence through loving the enemy is the most salient feature of this new model *polis*."[4] The call for a "countercultural community of discipleship"[5] is not unique to the Gospel of Matthew. Hays holds, for example, that Luke's vision of the church, "turns the world upside down not through armed revolution but through the formation of the church as a counter-culture, an alternative witness-bearing community."[6] Hays writes that Luke

> gives no evidence of the apostles seeking to reform political structures outside the church, either through protest or by seizing power. Instead, Luke tells the story of the formation of a new human community—the church—in which goods are shared and wrongs are put right. . . . The question that Luke–Acts puts to the church—then and now—is not "Are you reforming society?" but rather "Is the power of the resurrection at work among you?"[7]

The official social teaching of the Catholic Church, on the other hand, supports the position of Christian activism in the world. Many examples could be given to illustrate this point. Consider the following: The Synod of Bishops wrote, "Action on behalf of justice and participation in the transformation of the world fully appear to us a constitutive dimension of the preaching of the Gospel, or, in other words, of the Church's mission for the redemption of the human race and its liberation from every oppressive situation."[8] Likewise Pope Paul VI wrote, "The Church . . . has the duty to proclaim the liberation of millions of human beings, many of whom are her own children—the duty of assisting the birth of this liberation, of giving witness to it, of ensuring that it is complete."[9] According to John Paul II, the "motivating concern for the poor—who are, in the very meaningful term, 'the Lord's poor'—must be translated at all levels into concrete actions, until it decisively attains a series of necessary reforms." The pope is very explicit about the reforms needed. He speaks specifically about the reform of the international trade system, reforming the world monetary and financial system, the proper use of technological exchanges and the need to review the structure of the existing international organizations.[10]

The two views about the church in the world (the two competing ecclesiologies) are radically different. They also demand different forms of moral discourse. Hays' advocacy of alternative communities faithful to the Gospel depends on Scripture. His (almost) exclusive source for moral reflection then is the Bible. Moral discourse is then limited to narrative and prophetic. Hays does not attempt to make moral claims that transcend his community. His book gives no indication that he is interested in building bridges of moral consensus between his community and other communities. Thus he is not concerned with the second level of moral discourse, ethics and policy. Indeed Hays does not think it is either appropriate or prudent for Christians to be involved in this sort of discourse. He writes,

> If the church is to be a Scripture-based community, it will find itself reshaped continually into a closer resemblance to the socially marginal status of Matthew's nonviolent countercultural community. To articulate such a theological vision for the church at the end of the twentieth century may be indeed to take most seriously what experience is telling us: the secular polis has no tolerance for explicitly Christian witness and norms. It is increasingly the case in Western culture that Christians can participate in public governance only insofar as they suppress their explicitly Christian motivations. Paradoxically, the Christian community might have more impact upon the world if it were less concerned about appearing reasonable in the eyes of the world and more concerned about faithfully embodying the New Testament's teaching against violence.[11]

On the other hand, if one takes the position of the Catholic Church and advocates the reform of the international trade system, one cannot simply cite the parable of the Good Samaritan or the words of Amos or Isaiah and expect non-Christians (even Christians in decision-making positions) to respond with an "Amen." If one feels morally compelled to reform a social structure, perhaps through reading the parable of the Good Samaritan or from hearing the words of Amos, then one must appeal to justifications which persons, regardless of religious background, could agree upon. This brings us to the two second-level forms of moral discourse, namely, ethics and policy. Christian advocates of justice in the world must make appeals to the public ethical language and policy language.

Let's return to the dilemma in Christian morality discussed above. What is the appropriate form that Christian life should take? Should Christians work diligently to change the world or should Christians work diligently to form and nurture Christian communities? The solution is not an either/or. It is a both/and answer. Christians ought to form communities, for community life is an essential component of being a Christian. Likewise Christians ought actively to seek the well-being of those in the world. Justice is also an essential component of being a Christian. James Gustafson is correct in his comments on this. Concerning the role of the theologian, he notes that,

> The Christian community is not, however, the exclusive audience. Since the intention of the divine power for human well-being is universal in its scope, the historically particular mediums through which that power is clarified for Christians also has universal significance. The theologian engaged in the task of "prescriptive" ethics formulates principles and values that can guide the actions of persons who do not belong to the Christian community. . . . In effect, the theologian moves from the particular Christian belief to a statement of their moral import in a more universal language.[12]

This conversation is another level of the universal-particular discussion. Christianity demands both life in community, that is, partnership with others and the tradition as well as a universal concern for those beyond the community. The biblical message sustains community and continually pushes the community into broader spheres of human relationships. Recall, the image of the hourglass in our reading of the Hebrew Scriptures. God is the universal God that demands a particular response from followers. All persons, not just believers, are created in the image of God. The words of the prophets echo this universal outlook and yet provoke the conscience of believers. The Kingdom of God is more of a political image, the Reign of God over creation, than it is a metaphor for the Christian community. Jesus is not just for Christians.

The Bible is not explicitly for believers. Christian belief compels us to have one foot solidly in a fellowship with other Christians and the other foot solidly outside of this circle. It engages the world in dialogue and can find God throughout the world. Christians are thus compelled to move into the second level of moral discourse, to seek out others and make their claims intelligible to others.

The next part of this chapter will discuss formal moral reflection, that is ethical discourse. It will address the characteristics of ethics, summarize significant ethical theories, and relate biblical themes to the theories. The point of Christian ethics then is to bring the Christian narrative (Scripture and tradition) into dialogue with other narratives. Ethics is a primary way to proceed.

MORALITY AND ETHICS

The third of four types of moral discourse is ethics. Ethics, though one element of moral discourse, is often mistaken for the whole of moral discourse. It is common to hear the terms "morals" and "ethics" used interchangeably. Since they are thought to mean the same thing, or nearly the same thing, they are often thought of as synonyms. Alan Gewirth states, "This synonymy has clear etymological roots: the Greek word *ethos*, from which 'ethics' is derived, and the Latin word *mores* from which 'morals' is derived, both mean habits or customs."[13] Both terms have a common root meaning, but denote something more than that meaning. Ethics and morals also refer to reflection on social habits or practices. Morality and ethics can be both descriptive (answering the question, "What is going on?") and prescriptive (answering the question, "What ought to be going on?"). For precision of language, we need to specify the meaning of morality and the meaning of ethics.

Morality: Human Flourishing

The preceding chapters have given the reader a sense of what morality is about. We know, for example, that there are two fundamental questions of morality, "Who am I to be?" and "What am I to do?" We also know that these questions can be addressed to individuals as well as to groups. Morality then has two fundamental objects.

1) The internal characteristics of persons (and "cultures" of groups), often described by the terms "virtues" and "vices," "attitudes" and "dispositions," that is, the "being" question; and

2) The external actions and relationships between persons and groups, that is, the "doing" question.

If I were pressed to suggest a unifying description of morality, I would say that morality is about human flourishing. Morality has to do with fulfillment of what it means to be a person (both "being" and "doing"). It must be noted, however, that human flourishing is not necessarily the same as personal fulfillment. In many instances the two may overlap. However, a person may be satisfied and in a sense fulfilled or happy and yet may be lacking in a more whole notion of fulfillment as related to moral goodness.

The statement that morality is about human flourishing assumes a number of ideas. First, it assumes there exists some reality called the human person. It assumes that even though individual persons are different from one another in innumerable ways, there are some essential aspects of being a person that are in varying degrees shared by all people.

Second, this reality of the human person cannot be expressed in simple, one dimensional terms. The human being is a complex web of characteristics. Although it is difficult to fully specify "humanness," Martha Nussbaum offers what she calls an "intuitive approximation" of humanness. Her list includes: Mortality, human bodies (with their needs), the capacity for pleasure and pain, cognitive ability, early infant development, practical reason, affiliation with other human beings, relatedness to other species and to nature, humor and play, and separateness. She argues that two of these capabilities, practical reason and affiliations, play a special role uniting these characteristics.[14] Nussbaum writes:

> All animals nourish themselves, use their senses, move about, and so forth; what is distinctive and distinctively valuable to us about the human way of doing all this is that each and every one of these functions is, first of all, planned and organized by practical reason and, second, done with and to others. Human nourishing is not like animal nourishing, nor human sex like animal sex, because human beings can choose to regulate their nutrition and their sexual activity by their very own practical reason; also because they do so not as solitary [individuals] . . . but as beings who are bound to other human beings by ties of mutual attention and concern.[15]

One could add to this "intuitive approximation" of humanness a longing for, or an interest in, the spiritual. Humans are spiritual beings. "Humanness" is then a real but complex reality.

Third, the phrase "human flourishing" denotes growth and development. Morality is not simply about survival, although the numbers of our brothers and sisters around the globe living, trying to survive, is much larger than we are comfortable thinking about. Morality is not merely about the existence or maximization of these characteristics, but about their appropriate and proportional enhancement. As we are bound to others, morality is not limited to individual concerns about personal fulfillment. Human flourishing is a relational, not an individualistic, reality.

This description of morality offers a generalization about the nature and purpose of moral discourse. Moral discourse addresses the conditions for the possibility of human flourishing. Often the reason people think, talk, write, and preach about morality is in response to a perceived threat to human flourishing. Thus prophets often arise during a moral crisis. Disagreements on moral issues usually rest on differing conceptions about what is most fundamental to human flourishing. The real arguments among persons in a public moral debate may not only be the issue itself. The disparate voices often hold diverging views on what is most essential to full human life. The stories told by "The Entrepreneur" and "Constellation Earth" illustrate a tension that often arises in American public life, namely, are freedom, noninterference, and self-determination more crucial to human flourishing than community, responsibility, and fellowship? To summarize, if morality is about human flourishing then moral discourse is about the necessary conditions for human flourishing.

Ethics: Reasons, Distinctions, and Definitions

When the focus is shifted from morality as a general topic to moral discourse, that is, talking about morality or communicating moral ideas, the distinctive role of ethics becomes more clear. Ethical discourse (like narrative discourse and prophetic discourse that we have already discussed and policy discourse that we will discuss later) is a particular and specific form of moral discourse. An example from a concrete area of public moral discourse will illustrate the distinctiveness of ethics as well as its relation to the other forms of moral discourse.

Consider the ongoing health care debate in our country. Prophets, or persons engaging in prophetic discourse, have characteristically indicted the health care system (especially the delivery and finance of health care) in the United States as being unjust. Health care in America, they protest, is treated like a commodity. If you have enough money you can buy it, much as one can buy a car or a CD. Many people, however, cannot afford to buy health care, so they go without. Health care services ought to be, we are told, based on need and not ability to pay. Health care is a right that people have, not a privilege they earn.

An advocate for reform of the health care system might use a narrative to describe the real consequences of the unjust manner health care is distributed. Sylvia Ann Hewlett, for example, tells her readers the story of Cinde Guzman.[16] Guzman, a woman married to a student, works but has no medical insurance. When she gets pregnant and seeks prenatal care, she finds that all the doctors want a guarantee of payment up front. Guzman is caught in a bind because she makes too much money to qualify for public medical aid and does not have the $1000 needed to pay the doctor. By the time she saves the money, she is six months pregnant. Two nights before her first appointment she feels sick with cramps and pains in her abdomen. Her husband rushes her to the hospital where she delivers the baby. Guzman's baby, Carina, survives, but not without intensive care. Five weeks pass before all the tubes and wires are removed from her. Hewlett states Guzman's condition could have been diagnosed had she had prenatal care. The irony of this, Hewlett concludes, is that public medical aid that would not pay the $1000 for prenatal care, paid Carina's hospital bill of $150,000. Hewlett's narrative of Cinde and Carina Guzman is intended to spark the sentiment in the reader that something is morally and economically wrong with our present health care system. The story grabs our attention. Hewlett wants us to feel for Cinde and Carina as well as react to the distribution of health care.

Narratives are "prediscursive."[17] What this means is that while narratives do not contain analytical reasoning, they afford the opportunity for such reasoning. Narratives provide the moral sentiments or moral intuitions that lead one to consider a problem or issue analytically. The story of Cinde and Carina Guzman, for example, encourages us to think about the health care system. Is it unjust that in this country Carina would have to suffer needlessly? Or is the predicament faced by the Guzmans simply unfortunate?[18] In order to consider these questions, one must have some conception or idea of what "justice" means.

Thus there is a need for a form of moral discourse that logically examines the meaning of moral terms. There is, moreover, a need for a mediating language, a language that seeks to overcome competing narratives and to rationally reflect on the prophet's message. This form of discourse is called ethical discourse. Ethics seeks to build common ground and transcend particularities through use of reasoned argument.

Ethical discourse takes a more conceptual, analytical, or philosophical approach to moral discourse than the other three forms.[19] It is the task of ethical discourse to present reasonable arguments for moral judgments, highlight morally relevant distinctions, and offer precise definitions of moral terms.

Let's consider these three characteristics in reverse order. Ethics offers precise definitions of moral terms. If the prophet were to proclaim that all persons have a right to health care, the task of the ethicist would be to examine the notion of a right and to defend or reject the claim that all persons (or at least all citizens of the United States) have a right to basic health care. This task would entail a logical analysis of what it means to have a right and theoretical reflection on who has rights and why they have rights. If the ethicist rationally demonstrates that people do indeed have rights, she would then need to examine how the right to health care might relate to other rights, that is, the ethicist must highlight morally relevant distinctions. If the ethicist believes people have a right to health care, she would then need to describe in a clear, concise, and coherent manner what is meant by "basic" health care. Furthermore, the ethicist would need to offer criteria for discerning among conflicting claims and limiting cases.[20]

Throughout the entire project, the ethicist would offer reasonable arguments for the moral descriptions, distinctions, and judgments. If one were to disagree with a conclusion presented within the ethical form of moral discourse, the critic would have to enter the same arena as the ethicist. That is to say, the ethical argument made through analytical reason has to be challenged through analytical reason. This could be done in a number of ways. A critic might challenge the conclusions of an ethicist by examining the distinctions the ethicist relies on. Perhaps a particular distinction is arbitrary or unwarranted rather than logical. The critic might also challenge the assumptions or the grounds of the ethicist. Finally, the critic might find a contradiction or an inconsistency in the ethical argument suggesting that the ethical conclusion does not follow from the argument. The ethicist might have given unsatisfactory arguments for the position.

The four forms of moral discourse are connected in a variety of ways. There is often a progression in public moral conversation from the narrative and prophetic to the ethical and finally to policy. Gustafson's comments on ethical discourse hints at this progression. He writes, "Ethical discourse provides the concepts, the modes of appropriate argumentation, and important distinctions which lead to greater precision and stronger backing for what Christians and other religious communities think is the right thing to do, the good thing to do."[21] Ethics then, though a crucial part of moral discourse, is not the primary form of moral discourse. It is not the way people usually begin to address morality. Ethics arises rather, when people seek to demonstrate the validity of their moral positions or moral intuitions. It is then a second level form of discourse. Ethics ought not to be thought of as the most important form of moral discourse. It is one among the four.

TYPES OF ETHICAL THEORY

Ethics gives reasons and reasoned arguments for moral positions and opinions. It seeks consistency, that is, as it addresses issues it must make noncontradictory statements. If, for example, I say "X" about situation "Y," I must say "X" about every situation that is similar to situation "Y." Ethical discourse must also be coherent, that is, it must be logical. Ethics seeks a comprehensiveness rather than a piecemeal review of moral matters, thus a fundamental task of ethics is to offer a theory. A theory is a set of ideas or principles that direct a particular set of moral issues. This section presents a brief survey of the different types of ethical theories. Seven sets of ethical theories are presented.[22] The list is divided into two groups, namely, classic ethical theories, and contemporary ethical positions. The descriptions of the theories are not meant to be thorough, nor are they exhaustive. What is offered here is snapshot portraits to introduce the reader to ethical theory so as to provide a frame of reference for situating the biblical material in contemporary ethical discussion.

Classic Ethical Theories

There are four classic sets of ethical theories: Consequentialist theories, deontological theories, rights-based theories (liberalism), and virtue theories. I am referring to this set of theories as "classic," not because they have been around for a long time, but because each has had an enormous influence on modern moral thought. Although these moral positions developed within particular historical contexts, there is a timelessness to their claims that evokes the "classic" description. These positions invite continual discussion, interpretation, and critique. Their claims continue to strike critical themes in moral reflection.

The first set of ethical theories is consequentialism. Consequential-ist theories are act-based theories. Though many people judge moral right and wrong in relation to consequences, consequentialism as an ethical position holds that the only morally relevant, and indeed the morally determinative, features of actions are the consequences the actions produce. Consequentialism then judges actions as right or as wrong depending on their overall consequences. This is sort of a "bot-tom-line" mentality. Though most of us are not strict consequentialists, we often do justify actions based solely on their consequences. Think of examples in your own life where the consequences of an action determined for you whether an act was right or wrong. Pay attention to the news reports or read the newspaper for a week and you will see consequentialist arguments behind some business decisions and some government policy. The concept of an ethical *theory*, however, rests on the notion of consistency. One must be consistent in one's use of moral criteria. An argument that the consequences are morally determinative in one area would then suggest that consequences ought to be seen as morally determinative in all areas.

The most prominent form of consequentialism is utilitarianism. Although several forms of utilitarianism can be distinguished, the defining characteristic of utilitarianism is the principle of utility. The principle of utility holds "quite strictly that the moral end to be sought in all we do is the greatest possible balance of good over evil (or the least possible balance of evil over good) in the world as a whole."[23] The classic figures of utilitarianism are Jeremy Bentham (1748–1832) and John Stuart Mill (1806–1873).[24] Any argument whether moral, economic, political, or social that rests on the position that a certain act is appropriate because it produces the "greatest good for the greatest number of people" is utilitarian and thus consequentialist.

A second classic set of ethical theories is deontological or duty-based ethics. Like consequentialism, this set of theories is act-centered. In contrast to consequentialism, duty theories hold a different criterion of right and wrong. Put simply, deontological theories reject the notion that consequences determine whether an action is right or wrong. Some acts are wrong regardless of the consequences they produce. The rightness or wrongness of an act is based then either on the nature of the act itself (some acts can never be justified) or the act in relation to a universal moral principle (killing is always wrong). The most significant formulation of a deontological ethic is offered by Immanuel Kant (1742–1804). Indeed Kant is so identified with duty-based ethics that subsequent deontological ethics have been referred to as "Kantian," whether or not they directly rely on Kant's arguments. In *Groundwork for the Metaphysics of Morals*, Kant seeks and intends to establish "the supreme principle of morality"[25] which he states as: "Act as though the maxim of your action were by your will to become a universal law of nature."[26] In other words, in order for an act to be moral, you must be able to universalize the principle you acted upon. So if it is right for you, it would be right for everyone to act the same way. Kant describes this principle as the categorical imperative because it is morally required of all people. This imperative, he says, has the practical imperative: "Act so that you treat humanity, whether in your own person or in that of another, always as an end and never as a means only."[27] Any act in which a person uses another simply for his own pleasure or gain is immoral.

Many people in everyday practice call upon rules to consider the rightness or wrongness of an act. Many people also believe that some acts can never be justified. People who hold these positions in a consistent and coherent fashion would then be working from a deonotological position. An ethic that highlights duty, obligation, or the moral rightness or wrongness of an act independent of consideration of consequences would be classified as a deontological ethic. Two prominent contemporary Kantian writers and their works are Alan Donagan's *The Theory of Morality* and John Rawls' *A Theory of Justice*.[28]

The third classic ethical theory is liberalism. If consequentialism holds that the ends are morally determinative and deontological theories hold that duties are the primary concepts in moral reflection, liberalism rests on the notion that persons have rights, and that rights, the legitimate moral claims of persons, are the primary categories for moral reflection. Liberalism can be understood as that moral position, expressed in political, economic, and social ideals, defending individual freedom and autonomy. Such theories, according to Ronald Dworkin, "presuppose and protect the value of individual thought and choice."[29] Rights are the moral protections individuals have against the government and other members of society. The power of rights language is captured in Dworkin's often quoted reference to rights as "political trumps held by individuals."[30] The Bill of Rights to the U.S. Constitution is a good example of liberalism. Under these first ten amendments to the Constitution, citizens have a variety of claims, what might be thought of as zones of freedom, against the government. These include the protection of religious freedom, the freedoms of assembly and of the press, and the right to due process. Liberalism defends the individual, and in its best forms defends all individuals. A consistent liberalism seeks to defend and promote not only the rights recognized by law in particular societies, but human rights as well. Human rights are moral claims all persons have simply because they are human. The United Nations after World War II drew up a comprehensive list of human of rights. The preface to this list holds that "everyone is entitled to [these rights] . . . without distinction of any kind, such as race, color, sex, language, religion, political or other opinion, national or social origin, property, birth or other status."[31] The classic proponent of liberalism is John Locke (1632–1704). Contemporary rights theorists include Dworkin and Alan Gewirth.[32]

The fourth set of classic ethical theories, virtue theories, contrasts the above sets of theories in a couple of ways. First, virtue ethics is agent-centered rather than act-centered. It prioritizes the question, "Who am I to be?" over the question, "What am I to do?" As such, virtue theory is more concerned with moral goodness than right and wrong actions. Certainly the above three sets of theories could address the "being" question, and one could say that one's character is formed by moral principles, but virtue theories see the issue of character as the fundamental question for moral reflection. Second, while the systematic thinking of the above three moral theories comes relatively recently in the history of thought (the eighteenth and nineteenth centuries) virtue ethics is as old as moral reflection itself. The work of Plato and Aristotle, for example, belong in this set "for they talk mainly in terms of virtues and the virtuous, rather than in terms of what is right or obligatory."[33] Indeed, the concept of human rights, rights that all persons have simply because they are human, is a modern moral idea.

Virtue comes from the Greek word *arete* that suggests excellence or the perfection of a thing. Plato describes virtue as a quality of a well-ordered soul. He lists the primary virtues to be justice, wisdom, courage, and temperance. In later Christian tradition this list became known as the cardinal virtues. Aristotle does not develop or defend such a list, but rather defines virtue, this pattern of human excellence, as the appropriate mean between possible extremes in a particular context. Virtues are "enduring traits of character" that moral persons possess.[34] In either sense, whether one lists and describes particular virtues, or speaks more generally of virtue, the virtuous person is "one who is disposed by character to have the right motives and desires."[35] Such character traits lead, of course, to certain kinds of actions. Moreover, certain actions, repeated over time, form one's character. Virtue ethics is more likely to include the narrative form of moral discourse than the other three classic theories, especially as narratives can describe the particular features of an abstract account of a virtue.[36]

Contemporary Ethical Positions

I am distinguishing the following group of ethical positions from the classic ethical theories for two reasons. First, while there are perhaps other ethical positions that are worthy of note, liberation ethics, the ethics of care, and communitarianism have had a significant and enduring effect on contemporary ethical discourse. Second, all three positions are in one way or another critical of the classic theories. They define themselves against, and in a sense react to, the classic theories. Note also that I am referring to this group as ethical "positions" rather than as ethical "theories." The following ethical positions are characterized by serious moral reflection but do not have the same universality claimed by the ethical theorists. Indeed, the advocates of the following positions do not intend universality.[37] This intention is a crucial part of their ethical positions.

The first contemporary position to be considered is liberation ethics. It is the aim of liberation ethics to turn mainstream ethical discourse upside down. Originating in Latin American countries, liberation ethics, an aspect of liberation theology, is suspicious of the traditional ethical endeavor. Ethical discourse, as described above, claims a certain objectivity and strives for a universality, whether through a focus on ends, duties, rights, or the moral good. Liberation ethics, on the other hand, rejects the notion that moral reflection can be truly objective. Ethical discourse always and everywhere is a product of its context. Thus liberation ethics does not aspire to be objective in the abstract sense because it, by definition, arises from within the context of oppression. Liberation ethics then is an advocacy ethic. It claims partiality and preference for the experience of the poor. The steps, as it were, of liberation ethics then include a structural analysis of the conditions of poverty and oppression, a description of why the poor are poor. Moreover it demands that the oppressed be made aware of their situation and that they become the primary agents of personal and social transformation. Liberationists tend to cross the categories of moral discourse. They certainly rely on narrative and they are forthrightly prophetic. But in their attempt to be systematic, and through their attempt to explain the oppression to the oppressors, they also engage in ethical discourse. The strength of liberation ethics is in its descriptive analysis rather than its normative claims. That is, liberation ethics highlights the immorality of the oppressive situations, but often does not offer a comprehensive morality of how to change it, or what the social order ought to look like after the transformation (or indeed the revolution). The list of liberation ethicists is long and varied. It includes not only Latin American liberation theologians such as Gustavo Gutierrez, but also Asians, Native peoples, as well as women and persons of color.[38]

The second contemporary form of ethics is the ethics of care. Carol Gilligan's important book, *In a Different Voice*, brought the notion of the ethics of care into mainstream ethical discourse. Gilligan argued that women speak "in a different voice" about morality. Whereas men are more comfortable with abstract notions of ethics such as rights and justice, women are more comfortable with moral categories such as care, sympathy, compassion, and fidelity. These are relational terms, and the ethics of care addresses the one who cares as well as the one who is cared for. Morality arises "from the experience of connection and [is] conceived as a problem of inclusion rather than one of balancing claims."[39] Caring, from this perspective, is not a virtue nor is it an individual characteristic; it is a relationship. The ethics of care then concentrates "on developing the attitudes and skills required to sustain caring relations"[40] in distinction to the more traditional forms of ethics that are concerned with rationality, justification, and "decision making in moments of high moral conflict."[41] The traditional ethical theories, moreover, aim for universality and impartiality while the ethics of care is more relational and particular. Caring, however, is not just a feminine quality. The ethics of care holds that caring "is as much a mark of personhood as reason or rationality" and thus a purpose of moral reflection is to help develop this capacity in all persons.[42] Like liberation ethics, the ethics of care aims to give a voice to the experiences of those persons neglected by the classic ethical theorists. These approaches reject the simple "add women [or minorities, or the oppressed] and stir" recipe to reform the classic positions; they claim, rather, that these formerly unheard voices offer important new views to moral reflection.[43]

The third contemporary ethical position is communitarianism. Communitarianism is a political philosophy and indeed an ethical position that recognizes and prioritizes the social nature of the human person. In contrast to liberalism that stresses the individual and individual liberty, communitarianism argues that persons are formed and act within a complex web of relationships. Humans are not so much individuals as they are "persons-in-community."[44] Communitarianism defines and defends itself over and against liberalism as well as the individualistic tendencies of our culture. Communitarians take this critique to different levels. There is a continuum, a scale, on which communitarians can be placed based on their rejection or appropriation of liberal theory. A telling point here is the respective theorist's interpretation of human rights. The more extreme communitarians reject the validity of universal, objective rights.[45] More moderate communitarians see themselves not as rejecting liberalism and rights language but as building on liberalism's moral contributions, while at the same time aiming to correct "imbalance between rights and responsibilities" in American public life. If the banner of liberalism is individual rights, the banner of communitarianism is communal life and communal responsibility.[46]

All seven of the preceding ethical positions and theories deserve more consideration than they were given in this chapter. Since the details were skipped in favor of broad strokes, the reader might note that the theories seem more alike than different. There seems to be the possibility of crossover and blurred lines between the theories. Are not the first three theories, for example, all forms of duty theory? The first says we ought to follow the Principle of Utility; is not that a duty-based theory? According to the third, do not we have the duty to respect the rights of others? Indeed could not all the theories described above be reduced to moral obligations? These questions are valid, and if nothing else, they suggest the danger of such an oversimplification of ethical theories as presented here. A more detailed presentation would suggest the nuances and fundamental differences inherent in each account. Such differences might include the underlying anthropology (understanding of what it means to be a person) and the vision of human flourishing. Suffice it to say there are several characteristic forms of ethical theory. Each coheres around an organizing concept, idea, or principle. Each addresses certain theoretical base points in respect to this organizational principle, and each goes to great lengths to justify its principles and conclusions.[47] None of these seven positions specifically coheres around the theme of justice, yet all have developed an account of justice within their systematic approach to morality.

HOW DOES THE BIBLE FIT HERE?

How does the biblical material on justice relate to the ethical theories discussed above? A short commentary on each will help place the biblical material in the broader context of ethical ideas.

Consequentialism—The biblical ethic certainly looks to human acts and their consequences. It is better, after all, that the hungry eat and the sick are healed than that they suffer from hunger or disease. However, there is more to morality in the Bible than acts and consequences. There are other prominent moral categories, such as personal intentions, and the means one would use to pursue the ends sought. Moreover, the biblical message demands just consideration for the very ones that would be excluded in the calculation of the greatest good for the greatest number of people, the poor and vulnerable.

Duty—A consistent theme in the preceding chapters is responsibility. This notion, however, is different from the notion of duty found in classic deontological theories. In these theories, responsibility is founded on a consideration of pure rationality. In the biblical view, responsibility is rooted in the concrete relationships of persons and communities to God and neighbors.

Rights—Rights language is not biblically based. There have thus been different levels of acceptance of it by Christian moralists. Those who see the dominant task of Christian morality as promoting alternative communities tend to downplay if not reject the use of rights. Other Christians espouse rights as a public way to protect the interests of the powerless in society. They would hold, however, that there is more to morality, indeed more to justice, than rights language can capture. Rights language can be conditionally accepted as a way to protect the vulnerable in society.

Virtue—The Christian story has significant ramifications for the sorts of persons Christians ought to be. Jesus exhibited particular characteristics and dispositions in his life and his death (several of which, for example, forgiveness and enemy love, are not contained in the standard set of classical virtues). Christians, as followers of Jesus, ought to practice such dispositions. The Bible does more, however, than advocate certain character traits. It also advocates particular actions. Biblical ethics are an ethics of doing as well as an ethics of being.

The contemporary positions, like the classic theories, display some similarity to the biblical message. While all three have an affinity with the Bible, none of the three can hold claim to the breadth of the biblical message.

Liberation—This is a strong candidate for the categorization of the biblical message given the Exodus event, the words of prophets, and to some extent the teaching of Jesus. In some ways it is hard to find fault with liberation as a general theme; however, the category simply is not broad enough to hold all of morality. Not even all justice concerns are equivalent to the liberation.

Care—This seems to be an equally strong candidate, especially as care is related to compassion. Like liberation, however, the notion of care is limited. It might be better understood as a corrective or a balance to complement excessively rational understanding of morality and justice.

Communitarianism—This again is a very strong candidate. The themes of kingdom and covenant suggest collective and communal interests. It must be noted here that communitarianism is very different from a morality, as articulated by Richard Hays, that compels Christians to form alternative or countercultural communities in the world. Communitarians are looking toward the development of whole communities. They pursue the civil society and civil discourse in society and not exclusive groups within society.

This review suggests that the biblical message does not fit neatly into any one of the above theories. Jesus was not a philosopher. Neither were Amos, Isaiah, Micah, Hosea, nor Moses. The seven ethical theories presented above display a whole range of theories in ethics. They also display a characteristic of contemporary ethical discourse, namely, a drive for consistency and unity.[48] The richness of the Bible, indeed of the moral life itself, cannot be captured in a single theme or idea. Indeed such a task places restrictions and "strange cramps" on moral thinking and moral reflection.[49] An alternative view, let's call it a "conceptual" vision of justice instead of a strict "theory" of justice, would include some sort of synthesis of the dominant themes and a proportionate presentation of the concerns of the theories presented above.

The basic elements for such a conceptual vision of justice, gleaned from the above survey and comments, might be as follows:

1) An account of justice will look for results and consequences, but it will not give in to the principle that only results matter.

2) An account of justice will be framed within the notion of responsibility. Justice must be understood as a relational term referring to right relations between persons and between persons and institutions. Justice is the moral bond that holds relationships together.

3) An account of justice ought to include a consideration of human rights, "the minimum moral protection of persons in community."[50]

4) While it is appropriate to speak of a just or an unjust action, it is equally appropriate to speak of a just or an unjust person and a just or unjust law. Justice is about the "ethics of being" as much as it is about the "ethics of doing." It is also about individuals as much as it is about structures.

5) Justice refers to all and protects all. It has a critical eye turned toward oppression and injustice and thus in those contexts calls for liberation.

6) Justice must not be construed in an excessively rational and calculating way. It is constituted by compassion.

7) Human life is life in community. Justice is a bond that holds communities together.

Finally, we must be reminded again that there is more to morality than justice. In the words of Philip Selznick, justice "does not invoke the noblest human virtues—love, sympathy, courage, self-sacrifice; it is not a promise of moral perfection."[51] In traditional discussion of virtue, justice is but one of the four cardinal virtues. Yet, what would a human society look like if love and self-sacrifice were the rule without the adjudicating vision of justice expressed particularly in the values of fairness and equality? Justice holds a prominent and indeed a privileged place in any consideration of morality. Aristotle, for example, regards justice as the "highest of all virtues."[52] The next chapter will examine particular relationships and suggest characteristics of justice.

CHAPTER FIVE

A Conceptualization of Justice

Justice is a habit whereby a person renders to another what
is due through a constant and perpetual will.
—Thomas Aquinas

Justice is simply a requirement of reason, which in science
and in conduct alike demands that the same be said or done
with respect to instances of the same kind.
—William Frankena

Justice as fairness.
—John Rawls

The obligation to provide justice for all means that the poor
have the single most urgent economic claim on the conscience
of the nation.
—National Conference of Catholic Bishops

A methodology, a way of thinking, has been developing in this book.
It holds that one begins moral discourse with narratives and experience
and then moves to more abstract language. Abstract ideas, after all, do
not fall from the sky into people's books and computers. Abstract ideas
are products of reflection on experience. Ethics is the form of moral
discourse that works with abstractions. It aims to define, describe,
defend, classify, and justify moral ideas. The book began reviewing the
first Creation story in Genesis and has worked its way to the discussion
of ethical theory. There is still an interpretative piece missing in this
process. Ideas, whether from narratives or from theory, have meaning
to the hearer only if the hearer has some relevant experience with
which to process the ideas. I have found that in teaching ethical theories,
it is good practice to give concrete examples that illustrate the position
of such theories. This chapter will invite the reader to think about

justice. It is an exercise in ethics with the aim of conceptualizing the meaning of justice. We will begin with the particular and move to the general. To use the metaphor discussed in the biblical section, we will begin with the narrow part of the hourglass and move from there to the broad part of the hourglass.

UNJUST TREATMENT

The best way to think about justice is to consider injustice. In other words, justice is best reflected upon in its absence. (The Exodus story illustrates this well.) Recall experiences in your life when you thought you were not treated justly. Perhaps you received a grade on an exam much lower than you thought you deserved. Perhaps you were prejudged by another: categorized or minimized because of membership in a certain group or because of a certain characteristic you have. Perhaps you were not paid justly for a job performed. Children, too, have a seemingly natural interest in justice: While they do not complain if they get extra ice cream (or a higher grade on an exam than expected), they do complain that it is not fair if someone gets more ice cream than they do.

The experience of injustice evokes strong emotions: anger, rage, bitterness. And there are negative consequences to injustice. Injustice strains and breaks relationships. If you think you are not being graded justly, for instance, feelings of hostility might arise in you. You might lose respect for the instructor, the course, and indeed perhaps the educational institution in which you are studying.

Most people would translate the word "justice" as used in the above paragraphs to mean "fairness." To be just often means to be fair. Fairness is fundamental to justice but it is not the only moral claim of justice. Equality is another essential element of justice. As a teacher I have a moral obligation (best described by the term justice) to treat all my students equally. I cannot be biased or partial or prejudiced toward any student. There are many ways that this equality must be actively pursued. I must, for example, treat like situations similarly. If two students get the same percentage correct on an exam, I must give them the same grade on that exam. I must "distribute" the class discussion time as equally as I can. It would be unjust if I called only on specific students for participation. Yet in one of my most important tasks, it would not be just for me to treat all students equally. I am morally obligated to treat unlike situations differently. That is, I cannot give the class all the same grades regardless of whether they did the assignments. When I grade, I start with unbiased assumptions. I must approach each exam with an attitude of equality. Each paper has the potential to be an A paper. However, if I do give each paper an A regardless of content, I am not being just to the students. The students who wrote better essays are due higher grades than other students. It would be unjust of me to treat the differences as if they were the same. Justice implies both equality and fairness. It implies treating like cases the same and unlike cases differently.

To fairness and equality we must add a third general characteristic to justice. From the biblical tradition, we must include the notion of a distinct and determined protection of the poor or the vulnerable. One of the more compelling illustrations (I should say animations) I have seen on this aspect of justice in the last few years appeared in a most unlikely place, the Disney movie, *The Hunchback of Notre Dame*. As I watched the movie with my kids, I was not expecting the film's brief, but pointed, exclamation of justice. The lead female character, Esmeralda, is a gypsy. Her people suffer severe repression from the man who controls the law in Paris, Judge Frollo. The movie illustrates Frollo's attacks on the "gypsy vermin" as well as his repressive "care" for Quasimodo, the Hunchback. At one point in the movie, Quasimodo is tied up on a stage in the middle of the public square to be ridiculed by the people. Esmeralda climbs onto the stage to free Quasi, and Frollo orders her to get down.

> **Esmeralda:** Yes, your honour. Just as soon as I free this poor creature.
> **Frollo:** I forbid it.
> (She whips out a knife and cuts the ropes holding Quasi.)
> **Frollo:** How dare you defy me!
> **Esmeralda:** You mistreat this poor boy the same way you mistreat my people. You speak of justice, yet you are cruel to those most in need of your help.
> **Frollo:** Silence!
> **Esmeralda:** Justice!
> **Frollo:** Mark my words, gypsy. You will pay for this insolence.[1]

The picture painted in this scene is of a triangular relationship. Esmeralda and Quasi share a common bond with each other, their friendship and their vulnerability to Frollo. Their lives are under the domination of

Frollo. Frollo has the power and authority to do anything he wants to them. There are many opportunities in the film where he can respond to them as people, yet he continues to see Esmeralda, the gypsies, and Quasimodo as less than human. (The film, of course, goes to great lengths to illustrate the humanness and indeed the virtue of both Esmeralda and Quasi.) Esmeralda demands justice. She demands that she, her people, and Quasi be acknowledged as people deserving respect and dignity.

Justice questions, that is, questions of equality, fairness, and protection of the vulnerable play themselves out in all areas of human relationships, from the most intimate to the anonymous.

CATEGORIES OF JUSTICE

Ethical discussions of justice have traditionally described three types or categories of justice, namely, commutative justice, distributive justice, and legal justice. Aristotle and Aquinas, for example, discuss these types of justice. Commutative justice pertains to relations between individuals in private (one-to-one) transactions. Distributive justice refers to how the government ought to disperse social benefits and social burdens to individuals. Legal justice refers to the individual's obligations to society. This last category, legal justice, has not been used in recent time, perhaps because of its minimalist connotations. Persons might have obligations to society other than those codified in the law. In its place, commentators have talked about "social justice" to describe the broad range of social responsibility that persons have as members of society.

This three-part schema was developed when the major moral actors were individuals and the government. While to an extent this categorization is still helpful today, the complexity of contemporary human relationships invites reconsideration of these categories. Indeed, this three-part categorization of justice misses some significant relationships. It assumes, for example, that justice or injustice occurs only within economic relationships. There are many relationships between persons, not driven by material considerations, that yet still ought to be governed by justice. Friends and lovers can treat each other with or without justice. Thus there is a need for another category of justice, interpersonal justice.

While the move from the category of "legal" justice to "social" justice is helpful, the use of the term "social justice" is somewhat ambiguous. It has been used to cover a large area of human relationships and is difficult to define. The National Conference of Catholic Bishops, for example, states, "Social justice implies that persons have an obligation to be active and productive participants in the life of society and that society has a duty to enable them to participate in this way."[2] This definition merges two different types of relationships. The first clause speaks of persons in relation to society. Individuals have an obligation to contribute to the well-being of society. This is the legacy of legal justice. The second clause holds that society has the obligation to promote this, that is, to remove structures and social practices, such as discrimination, that prohibit individual participation. For the sake of clarity, it would be helpful to split this category of justice into two categories mirroring the two clauses offered in the bishops' definition.

Therefore, let "communal justice" refer to the responsibility of persons, groups, businesses, and other institutions to society. Communities have legitimate expectations for individuals and businesses to promote the common good. Social justice then refers to the role of society to develop and promote the conditions for the common good and the well-being of persons. Social justice is primarily corrective as it speaks up for and defends the powerless and poor in society. Thus we now have the following categories: interpersonal justice, commutative justice, communal justice, distributive justice, and social justice. But one more refinement is in order; namely, to clarify the role of distributive justice as a separate category. To associate just or unjust distribution only with public-private relationships, as does the traditional distinction, is troublesome. Distributive justice can, for example, refer to how businesses allocate income or groups allocate power. All categories of justice include a distributive component. Thus distributive justice ought not be thought of only as a separate category of justice, but as a critical component of each category.

The categories of justice are then:

Interpersonal justice—our responsibilities to others with whom we are in close interpersonal relationships (such as friendship and family).

Commutative justice—our responsibilities to others based on professional relationships, employment relationships, or relationships based on the exchange of material goods.

Distributive justice—the responsibility of society through the government to allocate its resources and spread its burdens fairly.

Communal justice—the responsibilities of individuals, groups, and organizations within society to pursue and promote the common good.

Social justice—the responsibility of persons to promote the well-being of the vulnerable (for example, the powerless, the poor, sick, aged, children, victims of crime, even prisoners), particularly though the critique of established social structures and social institutions.

INTERPERSONAL JUSTICE

A reflection on personal relationships, especially friendships and other committed relationships, offers an interesting starting point from which to begin a consideration of justice.[3]

Friendship and Justice

Everyone (I hope) has or at least has had friends. Friendship is a common experience among people. This shared experience is something of an equalizer among people. Even though you and I might not be friends, we both have had friends. We can talk about having friends and the meaning of friendship. This experience can be a common ground for us to consider related issues. I think, moreover, you would agree with me when I say that friendship is a good thing, indeed that friendship is necessary for human flourishing. Everybody needs friendships and relationships to be fully flourishing people. Just look around; this is empirically verifiable. Every healthy and flourishing person you know has friends. It is interesting to note the "lost story" of Jesus' friendships. Often these particular loves of Jesus are forgotten in favor of God's love for all humanity. This love, called *agape,* is often posed in contradictory terms to *philia,* the love of particular people. Richard Hays, in his exegesis of the Gospel of John writes,

> Jesus addresses his followers no longer as servants but as his friends (John 15:13–15). Indeed, friendship is explicitly given an important role in John's picture of the Christian life. Jesus exemplifies a special love for selected characters in the story: Martha and Mary (11:5), Lazarus (11:36), and of course the Beloved Disciple. Thus, within the comprehensive love of the Christian fellowship, John allows for and even encourages special relations of love and friendship in a way that no other Gospel writer does.[4]

If friendship is a condition for human flourishing, then it is a moral category, an idea demanding moral reflection.

Justice is an essential aspect of friendship. I have on countless occasions watched my kids as they've played with their friends. Many times these play sessions were interrupted or even terminated by claims that one child was treating another unjustly. I do not know how many times I've heard, "I'm going home and I'm taking my toys with me." This statement, even in young children, is evidence of how fragile relationships can be. Friendships do not just happen. They depend on "things," namely, particular actions, attitudes, and words. These "things" often take work. These "things" are the core of justice in friendships.

Consider what it means to have a friend. Paul Wadell argues that friendships are marked by three characteristics. "The first," he says, "is benevolence. If we are somebody's friend we seek their good and work for their well-being."[5] Friendship is not simply a state of being; nor is it merely a feeling for another. Friends do not simply like each other. They seek the good of the other. Friendship is an activity. A friend actively wishes for the best in the friend and acts on behalf of the friend. The second characteristic of friendship is that it is a partnership. In order for a relationship to be a friendship, it must be mutual. Friendship is not a one way street; the benevolence must be returned. There are many relationships marked by benevolence that are not mutual. A teacher may care for her students but her students may not care for her! Friendships are characterized by mutuality. The third mark of friendship, says Wadell, is that friends share "similar visions and ideals." They mirror each other's fundamental interests. "Every friendship is forged around some good that brings the friends together."[6] Our friends, while not identical to us, are like us in significant ways.

How is justice related to friendship? This might seem to be a strange question. Aristotle, for example, writes, "When people are friends, they have no need of justice, but when they are just, they need friendship in addition."[7] This tells us something about the relation between justice and friendship. Justice is a good, but a "lesser" good than is friendship. Yet this greater good of friendship depends on justice. There would be no friendship without justice. One way to think of this is to compare justice to a foundation of a house. Even the biggest, most beautiful house needs a strong foundation. Thus Aristotle continues, "In fact, the just in the fullest sense is regarded as constituting an element of friendship."[8]

Let's explore this. Think for a moment about what you expect from your friends. Think for a moment about what you "are due" from your friends. On one level you might say, "Nothing." If I expect things from them, I would be using them. I would be a false friend. True friendship does not put conditions or expectations on the relationship.

This is true on one level, yet on the other hand, what if you told your friend something in confidence and he told this to everyone he met the next day? Trust is a characteristic of friendship. What if your friend begins a tendency of putting you down in conversations? A friend respects the friend. What if she never returns phone calls? Friendship is marked by a constancy. Even as an adult, have you ever had the feeling that you just wanted to (take your toys and) leave a relationship because you were treated wrongly? Have you ever felt betrayed by a friend? A person could betray you only if some general expectations about the relationship were violated. A complete stranger could not betray you or be disloyal to you.

All of this suggests that friends do "owe" each other things. Friends are "due" certain things from friends, not material things but moral things, namely, patterns of action and attitudes. The expectations and responsibilities of friendship come from the very nature of being friends. A friend, for example, has an obligation (not from some external authority, but simply from participating in a friendship) to be honest to the friend. There are moral and pragmatic reasons for this. A lie, one small lie, can be destructive to a friendship. It can break the trust of a relationship and close the persons off from one another. If one partner does not return the support or the generosity or the commitment of the other, the friendship is at risk. Injustice arises in friendship when one partner violates a general expectation of friendship, a standard of friendship. Treating the other justly is a given, a natural part of friend-ship. Injustice gets our attention and often brings with it hurt, anger, and resentment. Friends treat each other justly when they create the conditions for friendship. Justice in a friendship, giving to the other what is due, is a bond, a kind of a moral glue, that holds the relation-ship together.[9]

Just Love

In her book, *Personal Commitments*, Margaret Farley offers a compelling view of that set of relationships, including friendships, that are character-ized by a deep level of commitment. This set of relationships would include marriage relationships, parent-child relationships, and close friendships. After reviewing shared interpretations of people's experi-ences of love in these relationships, she ventures a working description of love as "an affective affirmation which is responsive and unitive."[10] "The essential sign of my love," she writes, "is that I do the deeds of love insofar as they are called for and possible."[11] She notes, however, that this description is not sufficient. Alone it does not give us insight into how we are to rightly love the other. After all, she notes, we can love another wrongly. How could this be so? A father can love a son merely as a projection of himself. A woman could love a man merely for how he makes her feel. There may be love (strong affections for the other) in these relationships, but the love is misdirected or perhaps immature. In both examples the basis of love and perhaps the relationship seems to be the person's own self-interest and not the good of the other. How are we then to love the other rightly? Farley uses the moral category, justice, to answer this question. She writes, "The norm for right love is the concrete reality of the beloved."[12] Her description might seem abstract and perhaps cold, after all she is talking about love, but consider her argument. A just love (you might say "true" love) demands that we love the reality of the other person. We love them, as the saying goes, "for who they are." If a father merely loves his son as a projection of himself, he is not loving the son for who he is. Farley states, "A love that fails to affirm the child's dignity as a person worthy of respect and love in and for himself is a false love."[13]

A just love demands that we affirm at least two aspects of the person loved. First, a just love requires recognition of the reality of the person as a unique individual. This person I love is a person with special needs, desires, characteristics. He or she also stands in a unique and particular relationship with me. I love my four children "equally" but this love takes on a different form with each. Second, a just love requires that we see the reality of the person as a person and take into account the respect due the person as a person. Farley's words, though they seem quite evident, are nonetheless very important. How often have you seen people who say they love one another yet treat their "beloved" with less respect than they would treat a stranger? Basic human respect for the beloved ought not to be downplayed in relationships.[14]

In the nature of friendship, in the nature of love, indeed in the nature of any human relationship, lies vulnerability. The act of becoming friends involves becoming vulnerable. What I mean by this is, when I open myself up to you, I am hoping and trusting that you respond to me with respect. You do not have to. You can brush me off; you can ignore me; you can even put me down. I am vulnerable to you. The time-honored definition of justice as "giving to one what is due" implies this vulnerability or an unequal power relationship. Inequality is implied in the term, or better stated, the term "justice" implies restoring an equality or correcting a wrong or ensuring a right relationship among people. If I am to act justly toward you, if I am to give you what you are due, then I am in a position to decide or at least to administer something to you. The "ball is in my court," so to speak. But this interim before justice is enacted or restored also offers the opportunity for the injustice of domination and violence. You are vulnerable to my response. This vulnerability implies a moral status. The state of being vulnerable, of being vulnerable to harm, confers on one legitimate claims to treatment. How will I respond? To act justly is to confirm the bond that exists between us. Will I grant you the respect you deserve as a person? Will I affirm your worth as a unique person?

Farley's point, and I think she is correct, is that you cannot truthfully love another person without that love being formed and informed by justice. While neither you nor I want to be treated merely with justice by a friend or loved one, without the essential component of justice, we would not truly be loved for who we are. Farley's description of the "concrete reality" of the other, in other words, "who we really are," is also an important contribution to our reflection on justice. Justice demands the dual recognition of the uniqueness of the person as well as the fundamental humanness of the person.

Learning to Be Just

Susan Moller Okin, in her provocative book on contemporary theories of justice, criticizes these theories for, among other things, ignoring the question of how people become just. She remarks that the writers of these theories all "take mature, independent human beings as the subjects of their theories without any mention of how they got to be that way."[15] This is, of course, an intriguing issue. How does any one come to have moral qualities? Where does one learn to be just? Where does one learn to love?

Wadell answers these questions in his discussion of friendship. He believes that "Good friendships are schools of virtue."[16] Good friends draw goodness out in us. We learn how to love and how to be just as we build our friendships. If we learn goodness and virtue from friends, the reciprocal must also be true. We can also learn vice from friends. (Any parent will testify to this!) This indicates the importance of choosing and befriending wisely. Deciding who will be our friends is perhaps the most significant moral choice we make.

On the other hand, we must admit that friendships are not our first schools of virtue. Most people would say, I think, that we learn to understand love and justice first from our families. Okin agrees. The family is the primary school, as it were, for the moral life. The narratives of our families and the narratives of the lives of persons in our families teach us our first lessons about "giving to one what is due." We learn what it means to give. We learn about functioning within relationships in family. We practice understanding what it means to give another what is due and we carry these lessons with us in relationships beyond the family. As John Paul II writes, "It is from the family that citizens come to birth and it is within the family that they find the first school of the social virtues that are the animating principle of the existence and development of society itself."[17]

This is not to say that in lived experience all families are models of justice. A family can also be the place were injustice is fostered. Okin takes this concern very seriously as she claims,

> Unless the first and most formative example of adult interaction usually experienced by children is one of justice and reciprocity, rather than one of domination and manipulation or of unequal altruism and one-sided self-sacrifice, and unless they themselves are treated with concern and respect, they are likely to be considerably hindered in becoming people who are guided by principles of justice.[18]

Okin continues, "If justice cannot at least begin to be learned from our day-to-day experience within the family, it seems futile to expect that it can be developed anywhere else. Without just families, how can we expect to have a just society?"[19] To paraphrase a saying, "Justice begins at home," or perhaps better stated, "Justice begins in the home."

The distributive aspect of family relations can be discussed in issues of power, decision making, work outside of the home, and household responsibilities. Issues of fairness and equality are relevant here.

In the descriptions of friendships and other committed relationships, we see that justice begins when a person recognizes another person for who he or she is. This recognition of the other as a person, and not as an object or as a thing, is the beginning of morality and the genesis of justice. The reality of the other, the presence of the other in my life, causes me to respond, namely, to give him or her what is due. As David Hollenbach writes, "Justice is rooted in the fact that the very existence of a human person confronts the other with a certain 'ought' that demands respect and support."[20] This is the key point:

justice begins when one sees the other as a person, when one has compassion. If justice begins in the home, it necessarily stretches out into every sphere of human relationships.[21]

THINKING ABOUT JUSTICE

This reflection on friendship and committed relationships gives us a strong foundation to consider the nature of justice. It suggests five characteristics of justice and provides the basis for a definition of justice.

Characteristics of Justice

First, justice is a foundational, moral element of relationships. Justice is a bond, a moral bond, that holds relationships together. You cannot be involved in a true friendship if you treat the other unjustly. It is, however, not the only bond that can hold relationships together. We know that domination, manipulation, intimidation, and even abuse can keep people "together." A dysfunctional family can live in the same house! There are "bonds" other than moral bonds for a relationship. This is why we name "dysfunctional" families or "destructive" relationships. We know, however, that it does not have to be this way. Friendships, intimate relationships, and families ought to foster personal flourishing. Justice is the moral category to describe the conditions for that possibility.

Second, justice (or injustice for that matter) is not first and foremost something "out there" resting in some nameless and faceless social structure or cultural attitude. Justice (and injustice) begins in the hearts and minds of people. It is a matter of choice and personal determination. It is, to use more traditional language, a virtue, a habitual character trait.

Third, justice (or injustice) is expressed in and through action. The just person does not simply think about right relationships and giving others what is their due, the just person acts for the good of the other. The appropriateness of these actions as well as the moral demand arises from the nature of relationships.

Fourth, justice is not a one-time event; it is a process. A friend is not honest to the friend only on occasion. A friend treats the other justly all the time. This, of course, does not always happen. We make mistakes. Thus the fifth characteristic, justice restores relationships. Sometimes in a friendship, as in all other relationships in life, you have "to make things right." Justice determines what is to be done to repair the relationship.

Justice, then, is that personal trait, exhibited in both one's actions and attitudes, that responds to the concrete reality of another. It is the moral bond that holds relationships together.

Responsibility and Rights: The Moral Norms of Justice

The two main imperatives for justice are responsibility and rights. As justice is the appropriate response to the concrete reality of the other, responsibility is the primary moral imperative for justice. Responsibility, however, does not sufficiently capture the fullness of justice. The vulnerable, those whom something is due, have legitimate moral expectations and claims arising from relationships. I expect my friend, for example, to tell me the truth. Because we are friends, because of the nature of friendship, I have a legitimate expectation and claim to honesty from my friend. Justice does not simply counsel people to wait until others take their responsibility seriously. Justice compels people to act. Rights language is the appropriate form of moral language in the face of injustice.

These two moral concepts, responsibility and rights, are controversial. That is to say, there is considerable discussion about what responsibilities people have or ought to have and about what rights people have or ought to have. Indeed, this is the heart of the debate about the meaning of justice. We must then take some care describing these terms.

Our Contemporary Problem with Responsibility

In ethical discourse, we can speak of responsibility in two senses.[22] The first sense of responsibility refers to one's moral accountability. Is a certain action, for example, to be praised or blamed? Are we to hold a person culpable for a certain action? This is a legalistic sense of responsibility. Courts aim to assess, for example, whether a person is responsible for a crime. The second sense of responsibility refers to one's character. Thus we ask, is she a responsible person? Does this person exhibit the habit of being responsible? The use of the term "responsibility" in this chapter refers to both senses of the term.

The fundamental problem with the concept of responsibility in our contemporary culture is that we, you and I, see ourselves and our lives as disconnected from the lives of others. In philosophical terms we would say that our culture prizes moral autonomy. "Autonomy" literally means, self-legislating. It means that I have the authority to govern myself and make moral rules for myself. Autonomy means independence from other people as it promotes the individual, the self, as the center of each person's moral universe. Our culture promotes this and equates the autonomous person with the morally mature person. Autonomy is best expressed through making deliberate choices. What this means in terms of responsibility is that I am responsible only for whom or what I choose to be responsible for.

The opposite of autonomy is heteronomy. "Heteronomy" means to be controlled by external sources. In contrast to autonomy, it suggests the lack of self-determination. There is a tendency in our culture to confuse responsibility with heteronomy. The contemporary sense of autonomy then seems to clash with the notion of responsibility. Some people are uncomfortable with notions of responsibility or obligation for fear of the loss of the self, for fear of being ruled by another.

The biblical message described in the earlier chapters challenges the notion of the disconnected self choosing or not choosing to be responsible. The Creation stories describe persons by nature in relation to God, others, and creation. The image of God theme claims people are God's responsible representatives on earth. Jesus' life and teaching demand that Christians take an active role in promoting the well-being of others. The ancient notion of a viceroy is still helpful today. If a king wanted to rule an area and yet is not able to be there, the viceroy would rule in his place. Communication was very slow, so the viceroy had to use his best judgment to rule as the king would. This service is not strictly heteronomous nor is it pure autonomy.

If justice is "giving to one what is due," the fundamental question of responsibility then is, "To whom do I give what is due?" or, better stated, "To whom am I responsible?" The message of the prophets and the teaching of Jesus provide a very broad answer to this question, namely, "Everyone, especially those in need."

On the Problems with Rights

I stated above that rights language is the appropriate ethical response to injustice. Moral rights are claims resulting from legitimate expectations of relationships. While the notion of responsibility is limited in contemporary moral ideas, the notion of rights is expanding. Rights language is the strongest language of moral assertions one can make in our society. In an often quoted phrase, Ronald Dworkin captures the power of rights language. "Individual rights," he states, "are political trumps held by individuals."[23] In life, as in a card game, we want to win so we accumulate as many trump cards as we can. There is a tendency in society, then, to enlarge the list of rights persons can claim. The point I am making here, based on the biblical narratives discussed in earlier chapters and as a reflection on relationships addressed later in this chapter, is that we ought to reverse the cultural norms that rank rights before responsibilities. Justice includes both responsibilities and rights, yet responsibility is the key moral term.

Alan Gewirth, I think, best captures the nature of rights. He writes, "A complete rights-statement has the following structure: 'A has a right to X against B by virtue of Y.'"[24] We can then consider four elements to a rights claim, what Gewirth lists as A, X, B, and Y. Let "A" stand for you (the reader); "X" stand for freedom of speech; "B" stand for the government; and "Y" stand for the U.S. Constitution. An example of a rights claim would then be: You have a right to freedom of speech against the government because of the U.S. Constitution. When are such rights claimed? When the government acts unjustly, that is, when it interferes with your freedom of speech.

Rights language has come under criticism recently by some ethicists. Reflecting on this structure of rights, we can see the source of these criticisms. The first is the confrontational nature of rights. Rights presuppose a respondent, namely, a person, persons, or institution *against* which you have the right.[25] Rights claims are demands. People who make claims make noise. They shake things up a bit and challenge the way things are. Rights are confrontational. They are claims of power. Some ethicists are worried that rights claims are essentially anticommunity. That is, rights claims break the very bonds on which moral relationships are based. Justified rights claimants, however, note that the prevailing bonds are oppressive and violent, thus they need to be broken. The civil rights movement is an example of this. Civil rights leaders demanded equal rights for all members of society. In the face of legal segregation codes and laws limiting democratic participation in society, they called for equal rights. As you read this sentence, there are people around the globe who are being tortured, raped, killed, removed from their homes, and imprisoned without any hope of a trial because their politics or their religion or their nationality differs from that of the government or the military. The rights of these people, that is, these people themselves, are being violated. Rights claims *are* confrontational, upsetting, and challenging but that in itself is not a sufficient reason to reject the legitimacy of rights in moral discourse.

Consider another example. We all recognize instances of child abuse, child neglect, and child abandonment. These issues have become focal points of community concern. In these cases a parent does violence to the child by rejecting his or her responsibility to care for and nurture the child. The child has the legitimate claim not to be abused or neglected or abandoned. The child has the right (although the child may not be able to articulate these claims) to have his or her bodily integrity respected, to be fed and cared for, and to be materially supported by his or her parents. These are legitimate claims arising from the nature of being a child, being a parent and the family, and indeed being a community. Rights language protects children.

A second criticism arises with the specification of rights. What rights do you actually have? Commentators speak of at least three different categories of rights claims—particular rights, civil rights, and human rights. "Particular" rights are rights you have, given your status or your place in society. You have rights in the workplace or rights in the university based on your relationship to the business or university. You share these rights with others who are in the same position as you. You also have "civil" rights. The U.S. Constitution and law guarantee you many rights. Civil rights are rights enumerated in the law. You share these rights with your fellow citizens. Finally, you have "human" rights, rights because you are a person. You share these rights with all persons around the globe even if particular governments do not recognize such rights.

While claims of rights of the first two categories have been around for a long time, the third category of rights, human rights, is relatively new (thus the controversy) in the history of moral ideas. The most important statement of these rights is found in the 1948 "Universal Declaration of Human Rights" of the United Nations. One could ask why it took so long for this idea to develop. None of the great theologians and philosophers of earlier ages speak of "human" rights. The 1948 Declaration fits in a historical line of documents beginning with the Magna Carta in 1215. Yet the Magna Carta lists the rights of a certain class of people against the English king. It is not a human rights document. The Declaration, on the other hand, begins with, "Whereas recognition of the inherent dignity and of the equality and inalienable rights of all members of the human family is the foundation of freedom, justice and peace in the world."[26] What we have here is an expanding notion of "who counts" in concerns about justice. The movement from the Magna Carta to the 1948 Declaration is a move from defending the claims of English barons to the assertion that "All human beings are born free and equal in dignity and rights"[27] and that being human entails a set of justifiable claims that ought to be honored by all governments.

Commenting on the Declaration, Jacques Maritain wrote in 1951, "it is doubtless not easy but it is possible to establish a common formulation of . . . the various rights possessed by man in his personal and social existence. Yet it would be quite futile to look for a common *rational justification* of these practical conclusions and these rights."[28] Maritain cites an incident in the drafting of the document that supports his claim. He writes, "During one of the meetings . . . someone was astonished that certain proponents of violently opposed ideologies had agreed on the draft of a list of rights. Yes, they replied, we agree on these rights, providing we are not asked why. With the 'why,' the dispute begins."[29] It is this very lack of consensus on the justification of human rights that has caused critics to reject these rights as moral fiction without intellectual support.[30]

If there is a common equality among persons, if there is an "essential" characteristic of being human, as was suggested by Martha Nussbaum earlier in this chapter, then there exist conditions under which those characteristics can be wrongly violated. The 1948 Declaration and the committee of which Maritain speaks recognized this. I think they are correct in their estimation. The reasoning rests on reflection of what it means to be a human and the conditions that by definition would prohibit human flourishing. Human rights are, as Henry Shue states, "moral minimums . . . the lower limits of tolerable human conduct, individual and institutional." They are the "bottom corners of the edifice of human values."[31] If there is such a thing as humans, there are human rights.

A related controversy about human rights recognizes their validity but questions their content. The rights generally recognized as human rights by citizens in our country are listed in the Bill of Rights. The rights in these first ten amendments to the Constitution, guaranteeing freedoms from undue government interference, freedom of the press, of assembly, of religion, etc., are called "political" rights. The 1948 United Nations Declaration, as well as other sources such as the official teaching of the Catholic Church, have included another category of human rights, referred to as "economic" rights. This set of rights includes the rights to food, security, health care, etc. This set of rights is controversial in our country. The controversy is because these rights demand the positive action of others. The best way to protect political rights, such as the right to freedom of speech, is to leave people alone. The only way to fulfill economic rights, such as the right to food, is to develop economic systems, such as a system of food production and distribution.

This controversy between weaker and stronger notions of rights, however, is not ultimately about rights. It is about the scope of responsibility. Defenders of economic rights believe that a community has the responsibility to promote the well-being of members, especially when such members are in some way hindered in working for their own well-being. Those who defend only the validity of political rights do not think the government ought to be responsible for such persons, although they might feel a personal responsibility to help. The defense of these rights, and the implicit broader understanding of social responsibility, is captured well in the following quote from Pope John XXIII's influential *Pacem in terris*.

> Beginning our discussion of the rights of man, we see that every man has the right to life, to bodily integrity, and to the means which are suitable for the proper development of life; these are primarily food, clothing, shelter, rest, medical care, and finally the necessary social services. Therefore a human being also has the right to security in cases of sickness, inability to work, widowhood, old age, unemployment, or in any other case in which he is deprived of the means of subsistence through no fault of his own.[32]

In an earlier time, the right to food might have been thought of as an impossible ideal. Today, it is not. The food, the means exist. This, coupled with the demands of human survival, encourage us to broaden our notion of the legitimate claims of persons.

The final criticism of rights language is that rights merely enhance the "hyper-individualism" of our culture. Rights, after all, are claimed by an individual against others. They can become like "No Trespassing" or "Leave Me Alone" or "Give Me Mine" signs that persons wave against all others. There is a danger of overusing rights language, and there is the danger that rights language might advance hyper-individualism. Society, however, has more serious problems than hyper-individualism. As Michael Westmoreland-White comments, "Those who want free reign to torture prisoners or 'ethically cleanse' populations breathe easier when we do not defend human rights. Those who desire to beat or rape their wives, girlfriends, or children with impunity are happy to see the language of rights disappear."[33] Rights have a powerful role to play in public moral discourse. We can look at rights language as we might look at the use of medicine. In appropriate prescribed dosages, taken correctly, rights are crucial to the health of society. In the good society, rights are respected. A good society, moreover, is characterized by active responsibility.

COMMUTATIVE JUSTICE

Families are more complex than friendships. While families have an integrity of their own, they function within other spheres of human relationships. Families are not only communities of love, they are economic, social, and political units. As such, they are affected by and indeed affect other social institutions. Thus when people reflect on the relation between justice and the family, they consider broader areas of justice, namely, the justice of institutions and the justice of social practices within which families live. We often hear, for example, of the effects of crime, violence, and the drug culture on family life. The workplace, unemployment, as well as other demands of the market, including consumerism, have had indelible effects on the modern family. Social policy, institutions, and social practices affect the well-being and flourishing of families. That is to say, the justice of these broader areas of human relationships affect the conditions for justice within the family.

Most of the time we spend in relationships with others does not occur in friendship or family life. Living propels us into many other types of relationships. The second sphere of relationships to consider is that set of relationships beyond our friends, family, and committed loves. I am thinking about relationships to people with whom we have regular contact but are not close to (emotionally involved with), namely, relationships in school, workplace, clubs, teams, organizations, and so forth. It is within this sphere of relationships that we spend most of our waking hours. The "rules" of these relationships are very different from the "rules" of friendship and family. These relationships are based on employment and particular interests. They usually are a combination of voluntary and involuntary arrangements. That is, while you may choose to work at a certain company, you do not necessarily pick your coworkers and your boss.

These relationships fall within "commutative" justice, that is, relationships between individuals within society. The model for this type
of justice is an economic exchange or transaction between private
individuals.[34] "Private" here means that the "public" or society or the
government is not involved in this relationship. David Hollenbach, for
example, writes, "Commutative justice is concerned with the relationships which bind individual to individual in the sphere of private transactions."[35] The original context for this type of justice was the farmer
bringing his produce to the market. It would be unjust of him to
overcharge a customer or cheat on the weight or quality of the product.
Aquinas, for example, talks about "just price" for products as well as
the seller's responsibility for products sold to customers. Commutative
justice adjudicates conflicts that arise from "contracts or promises in the
sphere of private interaction."[36] Jon Gunnemann writes, "Commutative
justice is rooted in the fundamental moral prohibition against harm. In
exchange, harm is avoided when there is equivalence of exchange, harm
is done when there is not equivalence. The problem is to determine
equivalence."[37] The National Conference of Catholic Bishops, in a similar
voice, writes, "Commutative justice calls for the fundamental fairness
in all agreements and exchanges between individuals or private social
groups."[38] The example the bishops give is workplace related, fair
wages, and appropriate working conditions.

There is much to be taken from this traditional category of justice.
We are involved, perhaps daily, in private transactions with persons.
Yet contemporary life and its complex web of transactions call for a
broader understanding of commutative justice.

Beyond Private and Public

There is a crucial distinction between the traditional formulation of
commutative justice and complexity of economic relationships in contemporary society. Most of our transactions cannot simply be described
as being among private individuals. Take an exchange that each of us
has once or twice a month, buying gas. When you put gas in your car,
you are involved in a "private" transaction. You pump the gas and you
pay the attendant the amount on the pump—commutative justice. This
simple common marketplace transaction, however, is not so "private."
When you pump gas, you do not see the gas go into the car. How can
you be sure that it is gas and not water? When you pump gas, do you
really know how many gallons you are putting into the car? Do you

know that the gas is really 90 octane? Are you certain that the pump is accurately totaling how much you owe? We all trust the attendants and their machines. This trust is warranted because this transaction is not really all that "private." The government regulates the pumps (thank goodness) as well as what goes into the pumps. This "relationship" between the government and the consumer is not one way. A percentage of what you pay per gallon for gas is tax, federal tax, state tax, county tax, and perhaps local tax. The income taken by the gas station and oil companies is reported to and taxed by the government.

As we reflect upon the simple "private" matter of buying gas, we see that it is not so "private" at all. We could spend a good deal of time dissecting where each penny you pay per gallon of gas goes. Many "publics" and many levels of government are involved. Modern consumers and workers participate in a complex web of interactions within what appear to be "private" matters. The distinction between "private" relationships and transactions in contrast to "public" or relationships that involve government is not as clearly defined as it once was. While we are certainly involved in some "private" transactions, most of our transactions are mediated through institutions. When you buy gas, you "support" such things as the marketing strategies, corporate policy on hiring and promotion, pollution policies, etc., of the gas company. You also support the building of new roads and the repair of existing roads. The oil company you support through your purchases is probably a "publicly" owned corporation, that is, its stocks are available for purchase by the public. You may even own a fraction of the company you are supporting.

Commutative justice in the contemporary sense then includes a broad area of relationships, including relationships that bind individual to individual in private transactions as well as relationships mediated by institutions and regulated by government. We can define commutative justice as our responsibilities to others based on professional relationships, employment relationships, or relationships of exchange of material goods.

Justice: The Moral Bond

Earlier in this chapter, justice was described as that personal trait, exhibited in both one's actions and attitudes, that responds to the concrete reality of another. It is the moral bond that holds relationships

together. This truth about justice has become attractive to some interested in business ethics. I have heard, for example, people present the
following as a maxim, "It is good business to be ethical." There are
two implications of this maxim. First, if a business treats its customers
well, if the business gives the customers their due in terms of good
product or service, the customer will come back. This is commutative
justice in a narrow, but important, sense. This maxim also includes
relationships within the workplace, that is, the relationship between
employer and employees. The maxim holds that if you treat workers
fairly, they will respond accordingly. Justice, in this sense, is a moral
bond uniting seller and consumer as well as employer and employees.
Thus, "It is good business to be ethical." I think one can certainly argue
for this position, but it is more like a proverb than an absolute truth. It
does indicate that the realm of ethics, and more specifically, commutative
justice, includes external relations as well as the internal relationships
of a firm.

I am a bit leery, however, about equating economic prosperity
with being just. Justice as a moral bond may very well reap economic
benefits, but it also may very well require one to do something unpopular. Just as a family can be held through immoral means (violence) so
too can a business. There are at least two concerns here. First, the
workplace, or any institution, can be oppressive or exploitative or
operated unfairly. Given external conditions, these workers might not
be "free" to quit, thus they are in a sense stuck or trapped into working
in these conditions. Justice is restorative and corrective and indeed it may
challenge some unfair but accepted practices. Second, as the workplace
operates unjustly, it encourages that vice in its members. Institutions
play a crucial role in character formation. As Bellah, et al., write, "An
institution is a complex whole that guides and sustains individual identity,
as a family gives sense and purpose to the lives of its members, enabling
them to realize themselves as spouses, parents, and children. Institutions
form individuals by making possible or impossible certain ways of
behaving and relating to others."[39]

Justice requires that employees (and employers) be given their
due under the twofold concern of justice. First, employees must be
respected for their human dignity. Second, employees must be respected
in relation to their specific qualities and contributions. The distributive
component to commutative justice becomes clear here as pay structures,
promotion procedures, and hiring policies are matters of justice.

Justice: In the Hearts and Minds of People

In the traditional context of commutative justice, that is the relationship between the farmer and the buyer, the idea that justice is a virtue is easily understood. In the more complex contemporary economic relationships, the notion that justice is a virtue is a bit harder to understand. Virtues are characteristics of people. Recall the farmer selling his produce. Does he deliberately try to cheat the buyer? Only people are truly "moral agents." That is, only people have the capacity for self-determination that makes them responsible for their actions. When we consider the role of institutions in our lives, the picture becomes more complex. We say that institutions can function unjustly. Is this appropriate use of the term "justice"? I think anthropologist Mary Douglas is on to something when she argues, "The most profound decisions about justice are not made by individuals as such, but by individuals thinking within and on behalf of institutions."[40] Decisions that stockholders, managers, and boards of directors make on policy and employees have dramatic effects on people's lives and on the health of a community. Institutions, corporations, nonprofit organizations, schools, and churches are moral agents in an analogous sense: Institutions do not run themselves. They are run by and are supported by moral agents, "individuals thinking within and on behalf of institutions." But what is the proper response when governments, corporations, schools, or churches have unjust policies?

John Paul II, speaking on injustices as a sinful condition, offers an insightful and challenging view of personal responsibility in the context of social relationships. He writes:

Whenever the Church speaks of *situations* of sin or when she condemns *as social sins* certain situations or the collective behavior of certain social groups, big or small, even of whole nations and blocs of nations, she knows and she proclaims that such cases of *social sin* are the result of the accumulation and concentration of many *personal sins*. It is a case of the very personal sins of those who cause or support evil or who exploit it; of those who are in a position to avoid, eliminate or at least limit certain social evils but who fail to do so out of laziness, fear, or the conspiracy of silence, through secret complicity or indifference; of those who take refuge in the supposed impossibility of changing the world, and also who sidestep the effort and sacrifice required, producing specious reason of a higher order. The real responsibility, then lies with individuals. A situation—or likewise an institution, a structure, society itself—is not in itself the subject of moral acts.[41]

Responsibility lies with individuals. Injustice is not something that just happens. Yet individuals can get lost in or mask their responsibility by being members of groups. Being a part of large institutions is yet another way our contemporary culture downplays personal responsibility.

Commutative justice refers to our responsibilities to others based on professional relationships, employment relationships, or relationships of exchange of material goods. It includes buyer-seller relationships of traditional societies as well as more complex relationships within and between modern bureaucratic institutions. Injustice in this sense arises then when a contract or agreement has been violated or when some form of violence, oppression, theft, or abuse occurs. Some injustice is resolved though the courts or mediation. In this sense it can be said that Americans have a keen sense of commutative justice. Our courts are full of claims for restitution from damages resulting from broken relationships or fraudulent relationships. Commutative justice is a crucial element of justice, yet it is not the only element of justice. Indeed interpersonal, distributive, communal, and social justice can affect our understanding of commutative justice.

DISTRIBUTIVE JUSTICE AND COMMON GOODS

It has been suggested in this chapter that justice is developed and understood through relationships. The requirements of interpersonal justice, for example, arise through the nature of particular relationships such as friendships and family. I owe my friend honesty and commitment because she is my friend. Commutative justice is interpreted through professional relationships or relationships built on some exchange. I owe my students respect and fair treatment because of the academic relationship. Interpersonal justice and commutative justice deal primarily with personal goods and the good of individuals within the community. We are, however, more than individuals. We are members of communities large and small. The nature of being in community requires justice, and justice is the moral bond that holds communities together. The three remaining forms of justice, distributive, communal, and social are understood within our communal relationships. They deal with the various responsibilities of life in community and the common good of members of the community.

Distributive justice refers to what the community, acting through the government, owes individual members. It reflects on the allocation of social benefits and social burdens to individuals. Questions of distributive justice surround our lives and are the cause of serious debate. Consider the following: The state where I live is characterized by one large metropolitan area and large expansive areas that include smaller cities, towns, farms, and natural resources. State legislators are always debating appropriate allocation of funds. Which areas of the state ought to get what percentage of highway money this year? Which population group (seniors, the terminally ill, the unemployed, children, college students) ought to get what percentage of financial support from the state? These are questions of distributive justice. The government is morally obligated to distribute public goods fairly to promote the common good. Distributive justice then has as its object "common goods," goods often limited or scarce, that are not wholly "owned" by any individual but are necessary for human well-being.

Justice cannot be concretely understood apart from the context of the relationship considered. There are contingencies in every situation that make a difference. The key word offered by commentators on distributive justice from Aristotle on is "proportional." Common goods and social burdens ought to be "proportionally" distributed. Consider the example above. Funding decisions made this year have to be made with respect to the history of previous decisions and with an eye toward future possibilities. It would be impossible to state a once-and-for-all rule to follow.

Proportional distribution also refers to the allocation of social burdens. Communities have to solve a variety of unpopular problems. Where does the garbage dump or incinerator go? Which community or area will host the storage of nuclear waste? Who faces the burden of certain zoning laws? Distributive justice refers not only to the common goods, but also the inconveniences and sacrifices that are part of community life. It is in the realm of distributive justice to analyze the tax system. Is the tax structure fair? Do all incomes of people pay tax proportionately? Social benefits and burdens ought to be fairly and proportionally distributed.

It is impossible to develop a definitive list of universal common goods relevant to every culture.[42] Given our particular context and culture, however, I think there are at least four sets of common goods.

They are: fundamental human goods, public goods, communal goods, and procedural goods. The first set of such goods is fundamental human goods. This set includes basic nutrition, security (from the elements as well as from aggressors), and basic freedoms (for example, freedom of speech and freedom of religion). These are common goods because they are commonly valued by persons and they provide the necessary conditions for persons to flourish. Thus the moral imperative: Every person ought to have the minimal nutritional requirements met and basic security needs met as well as basic freedoms. The government has the responsibility to oversee the distribution of these goods. In a healthy economy, most people are able to meet their nutritional and housing needs. Society, through the government, ought to develop a "safety net" to those who are unable to meet these needs. It is the responsibility of government to ensure that freedoms are respected and that security needs are met. The absence of fundamental human goods is poverty. The interference with persons having these goods is oppression. Think about living without these goods. What if you and your family were not able to enjoy these goods but your neighbors had them in excess? These goods are the moral minimums, the cornerstones of human flourishing. They are also the grounds for the justification and explication of basic human rights. Fair distribution of these goods is a necessary condition for the good society.

The second set of common goods can be called public goods. This set includes parks, roads, the physical infrastructure of the community, the air, and water. Who owns these? In a sense we all do, yet no one really owns them. Public goods require direct action by the government to insure their protection and development. Decisions about these goods are best reserved for the morally responsible government acting for common good. We cannot count on market mechanisms or private individuals to fairly distribute playgrounds, streets, highways, and sewers; nor can we count on the market to protect the air and water. Public goods, if they are to be developed, protected, and truly public ought to be under the control of the organization that is directly responsible for the promotion of the common good, namely, the government. Repressive governments have characteristically distributed such goods unfairly. Rights language here is related to fair access to these goods.

The third set of common goods can be called communal goods. This set includes such elements as social tradition, the modes of communication in community, as well as the community's history, culture, and language. Distributive justice asks such questions as: How open are the means of communication (the airwaves, for example)? Who counts in the tradition and the historical retelling of the culture? Questions of fair distribution of such goods are harder to quantify, but are nevertheless vital for good society. An issue here is control of the social narratives, censorship, and communication. A first-line tool in social control is control over the access to communication—television, radio, phones, e-mail, etc. A less overt form of social control is control over social narratives. Who writes the history? Who writes the news? Rights language here is again related to issues of access.

The fourth set of common goods refers to the set of social practices and institutions that can be called "procedural goods." This set contains the practices of the general functions of society, such as law, political participation, and education. "Procedures are marked by varying degrees of openness and exclusion, access and denial, participation and domination."[43] A key term here is "participation." Are the channels of social participation open to all? Who can vote? Who can receive an education? Distributive justice asks such basic questions as, is the law fair? Do the law and courts treat similar cases similarly? There is, for example, some evidence that capital punishment is not "distributed" fairly in this country, that "race, poverty and geography determine who gets the death penalty."[44] Is there equal treatment under the law and equal access to the law? Distributive justice examines how the procedural goods are distributed throughout society. Systems may be in place that discriminate against certain groups of people. Rights here are rights to fair treatment and access.

Recall that there is a distributive component in each of the other forms of justice. Nongovernmental sources can also distribute goods justly or unjustly. In an attempt to address this concern, various writers have listed possible criteria for distributive justice. Regarding the allocation of medical care, for example, Gene Outka has suggested the following as possible criteria: Health care ought to be distributed based on a) the merits or the virtues of the patient, b) the social usefulness or prominence of the patient, c) the patient's ability to pay, d) the principle of each patient according to his or her needs, e) the principle that we ought to treat similar cases similarly. The latter two, or a balancing of the two, offer the most promise, he suggests.[45]

In economic affairs (especially as they relate to the workplace and salary structures), John Ryan suggests the following possible criteria: equality, need, effort, productivity, and scarcity. But he further argues for a criterion (in his words, a "canon") that includes, but goes beyond, the five. He calls it "total human welfare." For Ryan justice requires that the interpretation of the value of economic goods is never independent from human dignity.[46]

Both Outka and Ryan are doing ethics. They both aim to make reasoned criteria for moral judgments and convince others of their opinion. How do they do this? They first examine the possible principles of distribution, citing the strengths and weaknesses of each. They then make a reasoned presentation why one or more ought to be preferred. They defend their positions with rational arguments. Why is this important? Think of the alternatives. What if a hospital arbitrarily picked who would get health care? That is, without reason, it just decided who it would treat on any given day. What if a business arbitrarily determined the salary of its employees? In both cases the injustice would force an outcry. Then what if the hospital determined, on principle, who would get care based on sex or race or religion or education or age? For instance, only white men under sixty-five years old would get treatment. Or what if the business, on principle, would never hire a woman? Decisions concerning allocation of such goods are open to public scrutiny. A theory of distributive justice seeks to offer rational justification for such choices. As such it challenges arbitrary decisions as well as discriminatory practices. Analyzing patterns of the distribution of these four sets of common goods gives us an indication how just or unjust a community is. It helps us gauge the levels of freedom and opportunity, as well as oppression and repression, within societies.

COMMUNAL JUSTICE

Communal justice reverses the equation of distributive justice. To paraphrase the famous words of President Kennedy, it asks not what my community can do for me, but rather what I can do for my community. If the first principle of commutative justice is to do no harm, the first principle of communal justice is to contribute. Communal justice recognizes that while the government's sole purpose of existence is to serve the common good, it is not solely the responsibility of the government to promote the common good. All members of society have a proportionate responsibility to serve the community. Communal justice complements distributive justice, "each member of the community owes something to all the rest, and the community owes something to each of its members."[47]

When we speak of interpersonal, commutative, and distributive justice, we are usually speaking about responsibility to and for certain people. Responsibility in communal justice is harder to specify. With communal justice we are speaking of responsibility, not to individuals as such, but to the community as a whole. The responsibilities of communal justice can be explored through the four sets of common goods described above.

Fundamental human goods: Amitai Etzioni describes general responsibilities related to these goods as he writes,

> Members of the community have a responsibility, to the greatest extent possible, to provide for themselves and their families: honorable work contributes to the commonwealth and to the community's ability to fulfill its essential tasks. Beyond self-support, individuals have a responsibility for the material and moral well-being of others. This does not mean heroic self-sacrifice; it means the constant self-awareness that no one of us is an island unaffected by the fate of others.[48]

The production of material fundamental human goods (food, clothing, shelter) is not primarily the job of the government. It is the role of individuals and the private sector. Thus if a company produces a good product, markets it appropriately, and pays its employees a living wage, it makes a significant contribution to the good of the community. Persons and organizations ought to make broader contributions to the community. This can be done in a number of ways. Persons can contribute to charitable organizations; they can volunteer; or they can be involved in community projects. Professions and organizations ought to contribute their talent and specific expertise for the common good. Communal justice is perhaps best illustrated during times of crisis. People have a natural tendency to kick in and help those in need. They feel responsible for the well-being of others and the community.

Public goods: If the distribution of public goods essentially lies in the hands of government, the initiation of projects and the protection of such goods, however, often depends on the actions and attitudes of individuals. Individuals make the choice, for example to litter, to pollute, and to use resources inappropriately.

Communal goods: Communal justice entails an "ethic of being" as much as an "ethic of doing." This "ethic of being" includes a willingness to make positive contributions to the common good, as well as a willingness to tolerate differences and respect others. In a multicultural and pluralistic society with its wealth of different perspectives, peoples, and ideologies, this is challenging and necessary. Civility is a virtue. Think about public discourse as a communal good. Participants can control the attitudes and environment in which such discourse occurs. Communal justice in our society demands a commitment to dialogue and rationality but is not unrealistic about social tensions. It holds respect as a goal, but it will settle for tolerance (especially in the face of intolerant individuals). Amy Guttman writes, "A multicultural society is bound to include a wide range of such respectable moral disagreements, which offers us the opportunity to defend our views before morally serious people with whom we disagree and thereby learn from our differences. In this way, we can make a virtue out of the necessity of our moral disagreements."[49]

Procedural goods: Simply understood, communal justice requires that persons participate in society for the common good. For example, people ought to pay just taxes and be informed participants in the political process—minimally, to vote. Communal justice also encourages persons to be involved in intermediary institutions. Indeed this is probably the most effective form of social participation. "Strong communities," writes Philip Selznick, "are institution-centered. There cohesion and moral competence derive from the strength and integrity of families, schools, parties, government agencies, voluntary associations, and law."[50]

A final word on communal justice is that while it supports individuals and organizations, it always looks to the good of the larger community. It pushes smaller groups to see themselves as parts of the greater whole. The authors of the book, *Common Fire*, capture this tension between belonging to groups in society and participating in the common good of society. They affirm the importance of belonging to groups, or in their words, "tribes," yet they are critical of "tribalism." They write, "a sense of belonging and participation in a meaningful tribe is how we first begin to identify as a part of a larger social whole." We must, however,

> recognize when the virtue of tribe becomes the trap of "tribalism." As we are concerned with it here, tribalism exists whenever the rules for "them" are different than they are for "us." When we would tolerate "them" being treated in a manner we would not condone for "our own," we are living within firm tribalist bonds. Tribalism becomes particularly toxic when those we regard as

different and outside are subordinated, stigmatized, and perceived as either threatening or of no account.[51]

Communal justice is understood in the daily actions and attitudes that persons and groups have as members of the community. It complements distributive justice as it expects all members of society to proportionally contribute to the common good.

SOCIAL JUSTICE

Justice, as I have been describing it in this chapter, is understood in particular relationships. An underlying assumption of the discussion so far is that the external environment in which relationships occur is morally good, or at best morally neutral. What happens to conversations about particular justice when the contexts of those relationships are unjust? Take for example the notion of slavery. I am sure there were many slave owners who were recognized as model citizens, upright and just people, and contributors to the common good of local communities. One could say they were just in the relationships discussed above. They upheld the requirements of commutative justice on two accounts: they paid a fair price for their slaves and they treated them as local custom dictated. They also pursued communal justice as they produced cheap goods for the market. Having slaves maybe even allowed them to pay their nonslave workers a living wage. Perhaps the slave owners even shared their wealth in the community. But they were slave holders who, by our contemporary standards, would be utterly unjust.

What this example reveals is that the four forms of justice discussed above are not sufficient to describe the whole of justice. There is a need for a form of justice that has as its object not particular relationships but general patterns of social relationships and social interaction. There is a need for a form of justice that responds to, reviews, and evaluates (so as to defend, reject, amend) social policies, institutions, and structures. This is the realm of social justice.

Earlier in this chapter, justice was defined as "that personal trait, exhibited in both one's actions and attitudes that responds to the concrete reality of another. It is the moral bond that holds relationships together." It has already been suggested that relationships could be held together on nonmoral bonds—violence and the threat of severe punishment might have been the bond that held many slaves to their owners. Social justice demands that the concrete reality of the vulnerable members of society be respected. In the normal workings of government and the market, people with power are more able to control the outcomes. In contrast to this, children do not vote, the homeless have no economic power, and in times of war and unrest, the lives of innocent people are put at risk in the face of military objectives. Social justice looks at the big picture of social relationships from the perspective of the poor, marginalized, and powerless. It recognizes, moreover, that human choice concerning actions and attitudes is expressed in social structures and social practices.

An analogy from health care can help to describe the purpose and aims of social justice. Let's say you are not feeling well. You have some unexplained pain in your side. You can treat the symptoms, that is, take pain reliever for a period of time and be comfortable. Pain relievers, however, might not address the underlying cause of the pain. You will not be cured by treating only the symptoms. Perhaps you have a virus that simply needs to run its course. Maybe you have an infection that if not treated will spread. How would you know? You need to undergo tests to find the cause of the illness. If the cause is known, action can be taken to heal you. Social justice seeks not only to address the symptoms of injustice, but the causes as well. It seeks cures. While providing food in soup kitchens, it asks why are people without food? Why are people homeless? Why is there violence at this particular time in this particular place? Social justice is then dependent on social analysis.

The notion that society or particular social practices can be changed in significant ways is a fairly modern idea. Slavery is a good example of this. The abolition and nearly universal condemnation of slavery is a modern phenomenon. (Slavery, especially the sale of children, still exists around the globe.) Indeed the history of justified slavery is thousands of times longer than the history of the condemnation of slavery. For a variety of reasons, it was not possible until the eighteenth century for "thinkers to conceive for the first time of altering a large-scale social institution that was perceived as morally wrong."[52] There is indeed an embarrassing amount of literature in the Christian tradition justifying the institution of slavery.[53] Now slavery is condemned. No one has the right to own and/or control another human.

How did slavery end in the United States? This is a complicated question. I think it is safe to say that there were many persons and groups responsible for the end of slavery in the United States. This suggests another characteristic of social justice. Social injustice cannot be solved by individuals, private organizations, businesses, or the

government alone. The participation of each is necessary but not sufficient. Responsibility to address and resolve injustice runs wide and
deep. Responsibility cuts across society, thus the notion of "social"
justice in distinction to "personal" or "individual" justice. The formal
organizing element of society, the government, or the state has a
significant but not exclusive responsibility to address these concerns.
Indeed the government itself might be, and often is, the target of social
justice reforms.

Social justice takes precedence over other forms of justice. An
example of this is minimum wage laws and laws regarding working
conditions. These laws were developed to protect workers from abuse
by employers. They are the result of social justice movements. These
laws intrude into relationships usually governed by commutative justice.
The agreement of wages today between an employer and employee is
framed by minimum wage laws. Commutative justice is framed by
social justice. Social justice then is the responsibility of all (including
the vulnerable) to promote the well-being of the vulnerable (for example, the powerless, poor, sick, aged, children) particularly through the
critique of established social structures and social institutions. In the
concept of social justice then, we see the unification of two moral ideas.
The dominant justice concern of the eighth century prophets—how
the poor and powerless fare in society—is combined the modern notion
that social structures and institutions can be and indeed ought to be
changed so as to promote the common good.

EXPANDING THE SPHERES

There is a final area to consider within an expanded interpretation of
justice. The relationship here might be broadly construed as persons in
relation to nature. People depend on nature for life and, to a certain
extent, nature depends on humans for its well-being. There are some
important ethical issues here. Do future generations have rights? That
is to say, do your unborn great-grandchildren have moral claims on
you? Does a mining business have a "moral responsibility" to the land
after it strip-mines it? Do individual animals or species of animals have
rights? Does a bald eagle have a right to noninterference from you? Do
eagles have a right to be protected by humans from other humans? Do
sewer rats or snakes have any justified claims on persons? Is there a
moral difference between eagles and rats? Does your pet dog or cat or
fish have rights? These are important questions, but they are beyond

the immediate concern of this book. While I tend to think that nature, plants and especially animals, do have some justified claims against persons, I would use rights only in a limited sense. Discussions about animal rights have arisen precisely because humans have rejected their responsibility to creation. Persons do have responsibilities to nature. Certainly the first chapter of Genesis suggests this minimal moral position.

This chapter began with experiences that we all share, namely, friendship and love, and moved to experiences that many of us who have the opportunity to read this book have not experienced. Hopefully you have been immune from serious injustices such a poverty, exploitation, or oppression. If you are reading this in a college classroom, however, chances are that someone in your midst has experienced a serious injustice. The challenge here is to understand something you have not experienced. How do we do this? We start from our own personal experience "and then work to enlarge its sympathies"[54] Justice, though intensely personal, does not stand alone. It is a part of the moral moment when we see another as a person, a person like us. This is hard for us because we tend to see only those who are like us in obvious ways. We tend to see those who share our heritage or skin color or level of education or geographical location. But human nature is a funny thing . . . billions of people have it! Justice continually widens the circle of human recognition. It continually challenges us to see that justice in one sphere, on one level, is connected to justice elsewhere. As Martin Luther King Jr. wrote, "an individual has not started living until he can rise above the narrow confines of his individualist concerns to the broader concerns of all humanity."[55]

This chapter has presented a conceptualization of justice that included a discussion of the characteristics of justice and the types of justice. The chapter illustrated the role that justice plays in friendships and intimate relations. This discussion from common experience served as a foundation to explore the place of justice in broader spheres of relationships. Justice was described as the moral bond of relationships. Indeed as economic and social relationships are not buffered by love or commitment, the role of justice becomes more prevalent the wider the sphere. Responsibility was cited as the primary moral claim of justice and rights as the primary moral claim in the face of injustice. While justice is a virtue, a personal and corporate characteristic, it must be expressed in action. The final chapter then considers working for justice and the fourth form of moral discourse, policy.

CHAPTER SIX

Working for Justice

> The urgency of the hour calls for leaders of wise judgment
> and sound integrity—leaders not in love with money, but
> in love with justice; leaders not in love with publicity, but
> in love with humanity; leaders who can subject their particu-
> lar egos to the greatness of the cause.
>
> —Martin Luther King Jr.

MORAL CHOICE

Justice is but one of the cardinal virtues. Alongside justice in the
traditional catalog of the virtues are courage (also called fortitude),
temperance, and practical wisdom (also called prudence). Courage and
temperance are the virtues that direct our emotions so as to enable us
to act appropriately. We rely on courage when circumstances get tough
and things block our ability to do the right thing. Paul Wadell writes,
"We know we need courage whenever adversity confronts us. . . . To
have courage is to persevere in times of hardship for the sake of what
we love and do not want to lose."[1] Temperance "tempers" our emotions.
This virtue turns on or turns off, tunes up or tunes down our emotions
in proportion to the circumstances. Wadell writes, "If our emotions
are too strong, they may make us violent, they need to be tempered
down or subdued. If they are too weak, we are depressed or lethargic,
they need to be tempered up or aroused."[2] Practical wisdom, on the
other hand, does not solely deal with our emotions. It pertains more
generally to our reasoning ability. This virtue concerns the "capacity
for reasonable judgments about the means needed to attain our ends
in complex situations."[3] Practical wisdom has to do both with the
"means," the choices we make regarding our activities, and the "ends,"
the goals we seek.

There are three ways to construe the relationship between the
means and the end. The first, what we have previously referred to as

consequentialism, says that the ends are morally determinative. The ends determine the morality of an act. Thus the means are not morally relevant. If, for example, justice is the end we seek, this view holds that it really does not matter how we achieve justice. Violence, coercion, terror, torture, and abuse can then be "justified" because the end that is sought is justified. These examples illustrate the possibility of an incongruency and an inconsistency between the ends and the means. Given the view of justice described in this book, this position cannot be justified. As was stated in an earlier chapter, justice looks for consequences but is not ruled by the principle that only results matter. Indeed justice demands a concern for the vulnerable, the very people who might be violated in order to reach this "justice."

The second position relating the means to the ends holds the opposite view from the first, namely, that the means are morally determinative. The ends or the consequences are thought to be either beyond our control or beyond our concern. We simply have to act rightly and let the cards fall as they may. Deontological positions and some defenders of rights hold this position. This position is a bit more satisfying than the first; however, it too has some problems. Justice looks for consequences. If there is a situation of injustice, it demands change. Justice is restorative. It rights wrong relationships.

The third position is not merely a middle ground between these two extremes. It is rather a way of revisioning the relationship between the means and the end. Instead of separating the means from the end, instead of assuming that the means and the end are different realities, the third position sees the means as the "end in process." This view holds that there must be a coordination between the end and the means. The means must actualize the end. The means must have an affinity with the end. They must proportionately realize the end.

Let me give you an example to illustrate this understanding of the relation between the means and the ends. In our family we want to create a supportive and caring environment, as free as possible from violence and humiliation. With kids playing and teasing each other, this goal, of course, gets challenged every day. One day I was at home doing some last-minute work on the computer. While I was pushing to get the work done in a hurry, my kids got into something of a tussle in the next room. My immediate mental response was something like, "Stop fighting or I'll spank you!" Before I spoke, however, I recognized the absurdity of my thought. I was going to prohibit violence and teach my kids not to hit anyone by hitting them! The means that crossed my mind in this particular situation and the general goals of our family life were way out of line. If I want to promote alternative ways of resolving conflict between my kids, I had to explore such ways in my relationships with my kids. The means are the end in process.

Practical wisdom, the capacity to make reasonable judgments about the means and the end, requires discernment. It includes a familiarity with the particulars of a situation and bringing these particulars into dialogue with moral principles and ideals. Practical wisdom then suggests choice. I had to choose how I was going to respond to my kids. In this situation simply telling them to stop or laying down the law, "Do not fight," would not have been sufficient. I had to take concrete steps to resolve the tension.

People make choices, moral and otherwise, from within a variety of possible alternatives all the time. Morality is based on the idea that humans have freedom and knowledge to choose both particular actions and the direction of their lives. People can choose both the ends and the means. An anecdote may illustrate this. Our family cat, Biscuits, caught a wild rabbit in the garden. He trapped it and carried it around the yard. After we freed the rabbit from the grips of the normally sedate Biscuits, my son scolded him for being a "bad" cat. Biscuits was, however, being a "good" cat. He was doing what cats do, namely, hunt and kill smaller animals, and, unfortunately in this instance, he did it well! My son was assuming that the cat had the freedom to choose not to attack the rabbit and the knowledge that there were other ways of acting in this situation. My son was applying human categories and characteristics to the cat.

Cats do not have moral choice in the same way you and I have moral choice. We have a type of freedom and knowledge that are prerequisites for morality and moral responsibility. Thus when we speak of justice as a personal trait exhibited in both one's actions and attitudes, we mean that people have the choice to be just or unjust.

POLICY DISCOURSE

If practical wisdom suggests choice, then it also suggests policy. Policy is a determined pattern of how to choose. The term is usually applied to the practice of groups, institutions, and communities. Policy can answer both moral questions, "Who are we to be?" and "What are we to do?" Families have policies about, for example, bedtime for kids, dinner table conduct, dividing household responsibilities, etc. Institutions have so many policies that it may take volumes of books to explain them. The student handbook at the university where I teach contains over thirty pages describing university policy relating to student life. These policies include such concerns as discipline, sexual violence, sexual harassment, and use of alcohol and drugs. Businesses have similar policies. Policy directs decisions regarding the means so as to advance and actualize the desired end. Thus a criterion one can use to determine whether a policy is appropriate is: Does the policy undermine or advance the desired goals or ends? Given the concerns of this book, another set of questions must be asked of policy: How does the policy affect the well-being of persons? What type of relationships will the policy encourage?

Most institutions and corporations have their desired ends or purposes stated in mission statements. These statements define "organizational cohesiveness, identity, and effectiveness."[4] Mission statements may serve as a grounding narrative of the organization or may include a philosophical component and be analogous to ethical discourse. Mission statements generally include a vision of purpose (why we exist, our ends) as well as a position of strategy (how we will achieve the purpose, our means). Yet as proponents of corporate mission statements argue, "purpose and strategy are empty intellectual thoughts unless they can be converted into action, into the policy and behavior guidelines that help people to decide what to do on a day-to-day basis."[5] Policy discourse then is a critical and a necessary aspect of human relations and social organization.

Policies surround us and influence every part of our lives. This is not to suggest that all policies are good and beneficial. Some policies are oppressive. They can interfere with our lives and indeed frustrate stated goals or missions. We have all experienced having to conform with policies that just seem foolish. On the other hand, we all at one time or another thought that an institution we belong to, or indeed the community we are a member of, ought to have a law (a policy) about one thing or another. As a form of moral discourse, policy is very different from narrative, ethical, and prophetic discourse. According to James Gustafson, there are two questions that form the parameters of policy discourse. These two limiting questions of policy discourse are: "What is going on?" and "What is possible?"[6]

What Is Going On?

The first question the policymaker must address is, "What is going on?" Although this also may be a primary question for the ethicist, it does not necessarily have to be so. One of the most prominent philosophical books on justice in the past twenty-five years, John Rawls' *A Theory of Justice*, makes no reference to "What is going on in the contemporary world?" *A Theory of Justice* does not contain an analysis of the contemporary social context. Although rooted in a specific philosophical tradition, Rawls does not respond to specific injustices or to historical injustices. This, of course, is not characteristic of all ethical discourse on justice, but it does suggest that an analysis of "What is going on?" is not a necessary element of ethical reflection. On the other hand, the policy-maker *must* begin with this question.

Gustafson gives the example of people working on environmental policy. Persons involved in this area have to determine "the principal causal factors" of the environmental crisis: "Is it unrestrained human population growth? Is it pollution resulting from technology? Is it depletion of forest and soil? Is it the insatiability of human desires? Is it the absence of authorized power to legislate or regulate activity so that the values of environment are not depleted? Is it all of the above?"[7] An analysis of "What is going on?" must include relevant factors from a variety of different perspectives. In the area of environmental study, Gustafson suggests, "What is going on is not only a matter of scientific information but also of international economics, of political and international agreements and treaties, of political forces in both the northern and southern halves of the globe with their own national interests, etc."[8]

Policy decisions affect the well-being and flourishing of people as well as the conditions of human relationships. It is then within the realm of morality. Justice concerns ought to be included in the reality-probing question of "What is going on?" How morality is to be related to policy is a problematic issue. The American Catholic bishops give us a challenging view if this issue. They write that in the determination of public policy, "moral values are essential," however moral values and principles "do not dictate specific solutions." Morality, they hold, "must interact with empirical data, with historical, social, and political realities, and with competing demands on limited resources."[9]

What Is Possible?

The second question for the policymaker is "What is possible?" This is the question that drives the more prophetically oriented people crazy! A few years ago I invited a manager from a local corporation to speak to my class. I would say that he is a morally serious person concerned about moral relations within his workplace and the moral relations of his business within the wider community. I asked Bill to speak on his experiences. He gave several examples of moral issues he faced in his role as manager. He also offered what I would call his theory of moral leadership in the workplace. Bill's rule of thumb was "pick your battles." That is to say, he did not speak out on every moral issue that arose. His operative norm was effectiveness. Bill acted only on those immediate issues in which he thought he could be most effective. He was also concerned about being an effective moral leader in the future. Speaking out on every issue, he thought, would be counter-productive in the long run. He could be a more effective leader if he spoke out only on certain issues. Bill, in a sense, had a personal "policy" or strategy for dealing with morality and the workplace. His strategy was governed by a combination of moral seriousness and effectiveness.

I will never forget that class in which he spoke because a student, Chris, passionately challenged Bill on this strategy. Chris gave an example of an experience he had had with racism on a summer job. He spoke up at work and called the person making the comments on the carpet. Chris did not believe that one ought to sit quietly in the face of a moral evil or injustice. Knowing an evil exists and doing nothing in response to it is the same as participating in the evil. Chris' challenge was based on the ideas of personal integrity and authenticity. Bill was thinking and acting more from the policy form of moral discourse as he considered effectiveness and "What is possible?" Chris, on the other hand, was speaking more from a prophetic form of moral discourse.

This example illustrates the tension between the forms of moral discourse, and it reveals that none of the four forms is sufficient by itself. Bill's concern with effectiveness is rooted in his many years of experience working within a business. His strategy is valid. However, he must be careful not to lose the desire for justice in his concern for personal effectiveness. Bill must not reject the prophetic possibilities in his own life even if it might (or so he might think) damage his effectiveness tomorrow. Chris might continually remind himself of his audience. When I was student teaching, my mentor once said to me, "Know your stuff, and know who you are stuffing!" Chris would do well to remember this piece of wisdom if he continues, and I hope he does, to speak up in the face of evil.

MORALITY AND POLICY

The consideration of the relation of morality and public policy is complex and controversial. We saw one aspect of this in the conversation between Bill and Chris. Bill's concern for effectiveness and doing what he thought was possible given the constraints of corporate life infuriated Chris. Chris saw Bill compromising with evil instead of standing up for the moral truth. Compromise is a key word in policy discourse. The term suggests a movement or change in one's position to reach agreement or consensus with others. Prophets and people committed to specific ethical principles tend not to compromise. Savvy policymakers, on the other hand, realize that at times compromise is necessary to achieve at least some level of the good. The question of how much one should give up to achieve consensus is a major issue in the discussion of morality and policy. Another issue in this discussion goes to the very heart of the relation between morality and policy, namely, under what conditions can morality influence public policy? The next sections will discuss the various views of how morality is (or is not) related to policy.

Two Spheres Model

There are three paradigmatic responses relating morality and public policy, the "Two Spheres" model, the "Immersion" model, and the "Creative Tension" model. The Two Spheres model holds that morality and public policy are separate spheres or realms of human interaction and ought not be confused, mingled, or associated. Morality is understood here to be a private endeavor, while policy is a public endeavor. There are two very different approaches and reasons used to support the Two Spheres model, let's call them "Two Spheres I" and "Two Spheres II." Two Spheres I seeks to protect policy and members of the political community from the moral domination of others, whether the others be a majority or minority in society. Advocates of this position are suspicious of morally active people "pushing" or "forcing" their morality on the public. They defend a strong autonomy for public policy, free from the authoritative factors of religion and private morality. Government, they hold, should not and cannot legislate morality. The position is often articulated by civil libertarians.

There are certain strengths to this approach, but as a consistent position, it is problematic. The strength of this position is that it takes the differences between morality and policy seriously. They are different areas of human life and experience. Morality, as earlier suggested in this chapter, has to do with human flourishing in a holistic and comprehensive sense. It has to do with character issues as well as action issues. As chapter four illustrated with a discussion of the seven ethical theories and positions, people think differently about morality. There is valid disagreement among people of good will on moral issues. This disagreement is not only about how we ought to actualize the good, it is more fundamentally about the nature of the good itself.

There are, however, some weaknesses of the Two Spheres I position, at least as it might be held absolutely by persons. First, it must be acknowledged that all law reflects some understanding of morality. Richard Gula states, for example, that "laws spring from the experience of value."[10] Because we value freedom, he argues, we have laws such as freedom of the press and freedom of religion. Thus to state that "government ought not legislate morality" does not reflect the reality of legislation. Gula argues: "The state is legislating morality all the time when it comes to public moral values. Since the purpose of law is to promote public order, the state can and does use law to enforce moral standards which affect the public order. For example, homicide, rape, and theft are immoral actions which also bear legal sanction."[11]

The focus of the morality-policy discussion then is not whether morality ought to inform public policy but how it ought to inform policy. Or, to state it somewhat differently, how ought moral advocates present their positions to the wider community? Defenders of the Two Spheres I position must admit that the moral value directing their position is freedom. They too have a moral agenda. The position they hold highlights personal freedom as the primary value governing a good society. Advocates of justice must address their concerns in relation to freedom and at times challenge the notion that freedom is the exclusive social value. Unfettered freedom may indeed lead to injustice and be harmful to the public good.

For many advocates of the Two Spheres I position, the red flag issue is not that some people have strong moral opinions, it is rather that these moral positions are really thinly disguised veils for a domineering religious agenda. Here they argue, "What about the separation of church and state?" It is commonly held that persons in our society are not allowed to bring their religiously motivated morals into the public arena. This interpretation of the law is a misinterpretation of the law.

The First Amendment to the U.S. Constitution states: "Congress shall make no law respecting an establishment of religion or prohibiting the free exercise thereof." This amendment is about two issues, and thus commentators speak of its two clauses. The first clause, the "No Establishment Clause" is, "Congress shall make no law respecting an establishment of religion." The second clause, which is to be read to include the subject and verb of the sentence reads, "Congress shall make no law prohibiting the free exercise of religion," is called the "Free Exercise Clause." The first thing one notes in reading the First Amendment is that it places no restrictions on the activity of private citizens. The amendment is fundamentally about protecting freedom, not limiting public expression. Labeling the First Amendment as defending the principle of the "separation of church and state" is not wholly accurate. While the amendment distinguishes the two spheres, it does not separate them as the phrase "separation of church and state" suggests. The amendment is not intended to protect the government from religion but rather to protect religion from the government. It places restrictions on government activity.

The implications of this amendment are many. The government, for example, cannot force a religion on anyone, thus the ban against organized prayer in public schools. The government cannot favor one religion over another, thus the ban on Christmas manger scenes on public property. The government cannot punish people for their religious beliefs, except in extreme cases where the practice of such beliefs offers real harm to other people. The amendment protects the religious freedom of its citizens but it does not forbid "statements of religious belief in the course of public dialogue."[12] In the words of Stephen Carter, "It does not mean . . . that people whose motivations are religious are banned from trying to influence government," nor does it mean the "government is banned from listening to them."[13] The wall between church and state then is not impermeable. Carter writes that there is nothing wrong with the wall of separation metaphor, if the wall is understood to have a few doors in it.[14]

If the Two Spheres I position seeks to protect policy and members of the political community from the moral domination of others, Two Spheres II seeks to protect morality from being diluted by turning it into public policy. Two Spheres II is held by some persons with strong religious convictions and is something of a classic position in Christianity. It holds the world to be engulfed in sin, thus it would be "unrealistic to expect the laws of society to measure up to the moral standards of Christianity."[15] Christianity and society exist in a paradoxical relationship.[16] This position stresses that Christians, in their private lives, activities, and choices, must strive to be good moral persons. However, we cannot expect the platitudes of such a life to be legislated unto all. At times this position may lead to a "sectarian" view of Christianity in relation to the world. That is, it may stress the building up of the church or alternative Christian communities (see the comments on Richard Hays in chapter four) in contrast to the sinful world in which Christians live. This view may promote the development of Christian communities to the exclusion of concern for relations in the wider community and society. There are advocates of Two Spheres II who hold that the church and its individual members ought to witness a certain lifestyle in the world, a lifestyle that challenges the dominant patterns of interaction. Change in the world will then come about by others recognizing the truth and turning toward it. Like Two Spheres I, Two Spheres II promotes freedom as the crucial value for the moral society. Indeed religious people, especially members of minority religions, may be the most vocal supporters of freedom in the political world. Robin Lovin comments, "What characterizes those who have emphasized the connection between religion and freedom is their emphasis on the religious community, on its faith and the way of life that unites its members and distinguishes them from the rest of society."[17]

Again, there are elements of this position with some merit. However, as a consistent principle it too is problematic. The model offers a reminder of the sinful condition of human existence and the need to overcome and transcend this situation; however, this transcendence need not be limited to the Christian community. On the other hand, Christians ought to see their lives directed by the life, teachings, and death of Jesus. This model for the moral life, characterized as it is by such virtues as the irrational concept of enemy love and an impractical level of forgiveness, cannot be expected behavior of all people. Indeed Christians themselves rarely live up to these standards! Yet there is more to the moral life than these challenging images. Human flourishing includes the basic conditions humans need to live a life of dignity. Indeed a cornerstone of the Christian moral life is concern for the well-being of the neighbor, especially the poor. The Gospel narratives present a Jesus who spent more time healing people than he did in community with his close followers.

Michael Perry argues that all religions (not only Christianity) have an essential political character. Not only, he notes, do religions offer explanations about life and ultimate reality, they also offer ways, moral beliefs, to live a meaningful life. They are political in that they "comprise norms governing one's relation to others."[18] Different religions have differing levels of direct political involvement, but all have normative views on human relations. One way this concern is expressed is through advocacy of public policy that protects and defends human dignity.

Michael and Kenneth Himes frame this tension between the Two Spheres in terms of the distinction between the secular and the sacred. "Secular" refers to the temporal or the worldly in contrast to the "sacred" that refers to that which is holy, particularly to specific instances of the divine in this world. They argue the "Christian understanding of the sacred and secular is far more subtle and complex than any simple division of human experience into realms."[19] They describe a distinction between the sacred and the secular that acknowledges the universality of the sacred but does not identify any particular human expression with the fullness of the divine. The sacred, "is not some part of experience which is severed from the rest. . . . The sacred embraces human life in all its aspects, contemplative, active, marital, familial, political, economic, aesthetic."[20] However, "[n]o particular political platform, no matter how inclusive, no decision, however just, no action, whatever the nobility of the motive or the care in execution, is ever the realization of perfect goodness, justice and love."[21] This association yet distinction of the sacred and secular compels and directs Christian involvement in public life. The Himeses admit to the complexity of the move from faith to politics and hold that persons would "adopt differing strategies for implementing public policy appropriate to their views."[22] The universality of God and the comprehensive view of the moral life that follows from this expresses itself in many ways, one of which is public policy.

The Two Spheres model, in both forms, stresses freedom yet advocates an unjustifiable limitation. Two Spheres I limits government from listening to morally serious people. The argument presented here suggests that the wall between church and state has some doors. Two Spheres II places limits on the interpretation of Christian moral responsibility in the world. If God is God of all and present in all reality, then limiting moral concern to a specific realm is to deny something fundamental about God. The position advocated by Himes and Himes, and indeed by many Christians, rejects the Two Spheres response to the question of the relation between policy and morality as well as the opposite response to the question, the Immersion model.

Immersion Model

While the Two Spheres model, in both forms, demands separation, the Immersion model absorbs the law under morality. This position holds that civil law ought to be completely in harmony with moral law. The Immersion model, though held only by a minority of people in our country, carries some weight in political discussion. Some Christian fundamentalists are advocates of this view. They hold that the United States is and has historically been a Christian nation and thus ought to embody the fullness of Christian morality. These advocates usually rally around a Puritan-like expression of Christian morality that tends to promote what might loosely be called the issues of "private" morality, particularly issues surrounding sexuality. They focus on interpersonal justice and communal justice, downplay issues of distributive justice, and ignore social justice.

Christian fundamentalists generally have a conservative political agenda. There are, however, also people on the far left of the political spectrum who hold an Immersion model. Prophets, though often not involved in the nitty-gritty of the political process, might have an Immersion vision of how morality ought to influence policy. They may want nothing less than a society where there is no suffering, no violence, no hunger, and no war.

If the Two Spheres model promotes freedom as the key social value, the proponents of the Immersion model demand order. This view often begins with a presumption that contemporary life is on the verge of chaos. Recall the prophetic indictment. Listen to some of the public discourse. It tends to present a very pessimistic view of contemporary life. Christian fundamentalists argue that religion, specifically Christianity, can provide the needed order. Advocates of this view hold that traditional Christian moral values ("traditional" in this sense ignores the elements of tradition described in this book) are needed to provide the basis of a shared meaning, "without which even basic forms of civility and social restraint are jeopardized."[23] It is this Immersion position that the civil libertarians are most concerned about. In its quest for social order, the Immersion model rejects that notion of autonomy in the public arena as it promotes "a single system of meanings to which everyone in the culture may and must subscribe."[24]

In this discussion, I am purposely describing the Two Spheres model and the Immersion model as opposites, and indeed they are. However contradictory it might seem, some people hold both positions at the same time. This is an ironic point in American political life, and it reflects our collective ambiguity over the role of government and the meaning of human flourishing. For many fundamentalists, the Immersion model is demanded in areas relating to "family values," defined primarily in terms of sex and sexuality. As a group, they tend to be more proactive in the policy issue in this area. However, when it comes to more

systematic moral issues of poverty and economic justice, they tend to
have a hands-off attitude and promote solutions through such social
constructs as the market and established patterns of economic relations.
Warren Copeland describes this hands-on/hands-off phenomenon in
contemporary conservatism as follows:

> The libertarian strand believes that less government is better. They
> want to leave individuals free to make their own decisions within
> a free market. A second strand of conservatism, the authoritarian,
> does not trust individuals to make the right choice. They want
> government to guide or to force at least some citizens to do what
> is right. Even though these two strands of conservative thought
> are mutually exclusive in principle, most Americans who consider
> themselves conservative probably agree with each at different
> times. They want less government when it comes to taxes, environ-
> mental regulations, and welfare, but may want more when it
> comes to [such issues as] school prayer, and pornography.[25]

On the other hand, many contemporary liberals also have a split-
screen approach to the relation between morality and policy. While
they would continually defend the rights of individuals in all areas of
freedom in the personal realm (Two Spheres I on matters of individual
choice), they can hold the Immersion model or the Creative Tensions
model (discussed below) when it comes to government regulation
of industry. Thus they defend environmental regulations, workers'
rights, etc.

The critique of the Immersion model is implicit in the above
comments on the Two Spheres model. There must be a distinction
between these two realms of human experience. Shattering the distinctiveness of morality and policy harms both areas of human experience.
The problems with the Immersion model can be clearly seen in those
countries where there is a union between religion and the state. Certainly
the values of tolerance and respect for pluralism are at risk in this
model. Moreover, there exists the outside chance that the religious
morality might be positively influenced by culture. However, the longing
for community, the need for a shared language among the various
groups in society, is not an unwarranted desire. Indeed working to
develop a shared language in our diverse society, especially one that
highlights justice, might be one of the most important moral tasks facing
us today. Public order, like freedom, is a vital social good, but order

without freedom or justice is totalitarianism. This brings us to the third and final model of the relation between law and morality.

Creative Tension Model

The third paradigmatic response aims to balance the extremes of the Two Spheres and the Immersion models. In the words of Philip Keane, "there is no huge gulf between the realm of religious/moral values and the realm of public policy. Instead, public policy is to be acutely conscious of moral issues and it is to strive as far as possible to embody moral standards."[26] While there is not a huge gulf, there is, as the Himeses suggest, a distinction between morality and policy. The third model holds that morality ought to be in a Creative Tension with public policy. This model holds together a variety of seemingly contradictory ideas: all law is based on some view of moral values, but morality does not dictate one approach to policy; there is a certain autonomy that ought to be respected in the political area, but public policy ought to be informed by morality; if public policy ought to be informed by morality, morality and religion can also be informed by policy and the social reality. The Creative Tension model seeks to navigate between the exaggerated tendencies of the first two models, namely, moral positivism and moral authoritarianism. Moral positivism, a tendency of the Two Spheres model, holds that whatever is, is right. It confuses morality and law or morality and social practices. Moral authoritarianism, a possibility inherent in the Immersion model, holds that my way, or my community's way, is the moral way. The Creative Tension model tries to avoid these dangers through two fundamental presuppositions. The first is that public dialogue is necessary and possible. The second is that public policy proposals made from a moral perspective "must pass through what has been called a 'prism of feasibility.'"[27]

The Creative Tension model is optimistic that within our pluralistic society people can talk. When people talk about life in society, about what the good society might look like, there exists the real possibility for some reasonable consensus. Advocates of the Creative Tension model do not necessarily believe that dialogue is automatic or even that it is easy. Thus they often discuss the conditions necessary for this dialogue to occur.

Think of instances or relationships in your own life where dialogue does not exist or does not seem possible. You know that things in the relationship, first and foremost people's attitudes, must change before dialogue can begin or can be restored. There are some similarities between interpersonal dialogue and public dialogue. What conditions are necessary for people of diverse religions to enter serious public dialogue? Michael Perry's work is helpful here. He believes that persons from differing religious traditions ought not abandon their moral insights at the door of public conversation, especially conversation on policy. Perry, citing J. Bryan Hehir, believes that religious communities ought to probe their "commitments deeply and broadly enough" to "translate their best insights to others."[28] Note the word "translate." If these religiously based moral ideas are helpful for understanding the human good, they can be "translated" to wider audiences. Indeed as Robin Lovin has suggested, religions have a special and unique responsibility to strengthen public dialogue.[29] In this dialogue, religions have to recognize the pluralism of our society and be open to external challenges as they attempt to articulate their normative understanding of human relations within the wider community.

Perry describes two conditions for this translation of moral beliefs based on religious commitments to moral beliefs open to more public scrutiny. He refers to these as the "cardinal dialogic virtues: public intelligibility and public accessibility."[30] Public intelligibility "is the habit of trying to elaborate one's position in a manner intelligible or comprehensible to those who speak a different religious or moral language—to the point of translating one's position, to the extent possible, to a shared ('mediating') language."[31] The virtue of public accessibility "is the habit of trying to defend one's position in a manner neither sectarian nor authoritarian."[32] Perry readily admits that if one renders one's religiously based view publicly intelligible and publicly accessible that argument and disagreement (not to mention misunderstandings) will not automatically stop. That, he says, is not the point. The point is that "failure to honor a standard like that of public accessibility dooms argument in the public square, including religious argument, to play a role that is anything but constructive; it dooms such argument to play at best a marginal and ineffective, and sometimes even divisive role."[33] If a person arguing from a religious point of view is to be effective and offer constructive elements to broader pluralistic dialogue, that person must respect the notions of intelligibility and accessibility. However, even if consensus does not occur, the dialogue itself is important. Through dialogue the person meets others and, ironically, through this exchange, persons learn more about themselves. With dialogue comes the promise of community.[34]

Along with the hope in dialogue, adherents to the Creative Tension view between morality and policy also have a realistic vision of what elements of morality can or should be encoded into policy. The Himeses write,

> Essentially, public policy proposals must pass through what has been called a "prism of feasibility." This entails consideration of four factors: the good of personal freedom which may be restricted, the factor of equity in the burdens created by the policy, consensus on the need for policy in order to maintain public order, and the enforceability of any decision.[35]

The feasibility prism cuts both ways and thus promotes a notion of a proportionate level of morality in law. First it recognizes that, "there are many moral wrongs which are not best dealt with through public policy."[36] More significantly, it recognizes an openness to compromise as at times a policy "accomplishes a reasonable but only partial good" given the current political climate.[37] In this view, institutions, including the government, have a responsibility to promote the common good within their competence and areas of influence. Government and public policy ought to promote justice, secure freedom, and maintain order.

The Two Spheres model, in both forms, and the Immersion model have an affinity with narrative and prophetic discourse. As narratives are community based, they can support a separatist or isolationist view of Christianity. Narratives can also be understood in an exclusivistic sense or even tyrannical way indicating a dominance over all other narratives. The Creative Tension model has most affinity with ethical discourse as it seeks to infuse (not ignore or dominate) justice into policy considerations. In public policy, it affirms the dignity of the vulnerable across the realms of justice. This idealism is tempered by an acknowledgment of limitations. The Creative Tension model expects Christian involvement in the public realm. To reject such involvement is to reject a required area of human responsibility. The strength of the Creative Tension model lies in its presuppositions of dialogue and feasibility. The weakness of the approach is that it does not present persons with a clear-cut, black-and-white picture of how morality ought to influence policy. When is compromise permissible, when is it selling out? Compared to the extreme positions of the Two Spheres and Immersion models, the Creative Tension model must rely on the realities of the particular context to actualize justice—as best it can. It requires practical wisdom and patience to discern both the appropriate moral end and the proportionate moral means in the situation. To defend a policy that is morally rooted but not feasible is to promote a bad policy. It is never wrong, however, to defend the morality on which such a law might be based.

THE MORAL IMPLICATIONS OF POLICY

The section above has suggested that there is a dynamic relationship between morality and law. This is not to say that all morality ought to be made into law nor is it to say that all law is moral. This conclusion, however, raises another interesting set of questions. Namely, what are the moral implications of policy? Recall the two foundation questions of the moral life, "What am I to do?" and "Who am I to be?" While policy certainly directs action, is it possible to say that policy can make people just? Is it more realistic to say that policy can merely limit injustice? Consider the words of Martin Luther King Jr., the most prominent twentieth century American to challenge the legal structure from a moral perspective. In a speech on racial justice King said:

> We must continue our struggle through legalism and legislation. There are those who contend that integration can come only through education, for no other reason than that morals cannot be legislated. I choose, however, to be dialectical at this point. It is neither education nor legislation; it is both legislation and education. I quite agree that it is impossible to change a man's internal feelings merely through law. But this really is not the intention of the law. The law does not seek to change one's internal feelings; it seeks rather to control the external effects of those internal feelings. For instance, the law cannot make a man love—religion and education must do that—but it can control his efforts to lynch. So in order to control the external effects of prejudiced internal feelings, we must continue to struggle through legislation.[38]

King's view in this quotation suggests that the purpose of law is to control evil. Policy does not provide an answer to the question, "What ought I to do?" so much as it tells us something we should not do, in this case, we should not lynch people. There is nothing morally uplifting here. King is correct when he states that simply enacting a law will not change a person's moral character. In this sense, then, the saying, "You cannot legislate morality" is true. However there are very real ways in which policies do affect the moral outlook of persons and the moral context of a culture, a community, or an institution. In many of his speeches King describes the effects of segregation laws on African-Americans. In what is perhaps the most moving example here, he writes with controlled frustration in response to those who urge him to slow the civil rights movement. After describing a range of indignities and insults that he has experienced as a black man, he explains why he cannot simply wait for change:

> When you suddenly find your tongue twisted and your speech stammering as you seek to explain to your six-year-old daughter why she can't go to the public amusement park that has just been advertised on television, and see the tears welling up in her little eyes when she is told that Funtown is closed to colored children and see the depressing clouds of inferiority begin to form in her little mental sky, and see her begin to distort her little personality by unconsciously developing a bitterness toward white people.[39]

Enacting a law may not change a person's disposition, but a policy, especially if held over a time, can foster moral and immoral attitudes. King's example clearly illustrates how a policy, in this case segregation, affects persons. Policy, held over time, becomes part of the social narrative that forms and informs people. The segregation laws, no doubt, also formed the "little mental skies" of many white children filling them with superiority and racist attitudes. King states, "The habits, if not the hearts of people, have been and are being altered everyday by legislative acts, judicial decisions and executive orders. Let us not be misled by those who argue that segregation cannot be ended by the force of law."[40]

Centuries ago, in a time much different from our own, Thomas Aquinas wrote, "The purpose of human law is to lead men to virtue, not suddenly but gradually."[41] Aquinas seems a bit more optimistic on the role of law than does King, but Aquinas is not unrealistic. He also acknowledges that strict or burdensome laws may invite contempt in persons and indeed make them worse and not better people! Consider Aquinas' emphasis use of the word "gradually." It is not an unfair question to ask whether the civil rights laws passed during King's era have changed the attitudes of persons today. Certainly racism is alive and well in this country, but has there been any improvements in this area because of public policy? This is probably impossible to measure, but many people would say at least conditionally that civil rights laws have gradually slowed the evils of racism. King is right as he suggests that law cannot make persons love one another, but perhaps gradually, law might lead to a toleration, if not outright respect, for members of society who have been historically discriminated against. Over time policy becomes part of the cultural narrative. Perhaps ever so slowly, if policy decisions are informed by justice, unjust structures and patterns of human interaction will change. Perhaps persons living or working within these policies might also change. Policies might lead persons, albeit gradually, to virtue.

Moral ideals, principles, and virtues, if truly held by persons and groups, are naturally expressed through choices. Policy, a formal type of choice, then, reflects the values, either implicitly or explicitly, of the policymakers. Policy, moreover, affects the lives of people in many, many ways. Because of this, policy falls within the confines of moral discourse. Like the other three forms, it does not stand in isolation. Ethical discourse leads to concretization in policy, and as policy is tied to a specific context, it will be outdated and open to the criticism of prophets. Nevertheless, morally serious persons must place a high value on relating moral concerns, especially justice, to their policy decision-making capacities, whether as members of groups, institutions, or society.

DO JUSTICE

This book has had two purposes. It has described James Gustafson's four forms of moral discourse, namely, narrative, prophetic, ethical, and policy. It also has presented a view of justice, a way of thinking about justice, based on biblical narratives and reflection on the common experiences of friendship, family, and other relationships. These final pages will consider the dominant themes of this book and offer some concluding remarks.

Narrative and Justice

This book has suggested, in line with Gustafson's work, that each of the four forms of moral discourse is necessary but none alone is sufficient. Each of the four has its particular role to play in moral communication but that by itself, each is inadequate. There is more to moral discourse than can be captured by each form.

Narrative is the fundamental form of moral conversation. It is fundamental because of its power and its pervasiveness. Stories, songs, the witnesses of peoples' lives, art, cultural expectations, rituals, and so on, are narratives. To say they are "necessary" means they are essential. This, of course, is quite obvious. It is hard to imagine human existence without stories! Recall the qualities of a good narrative. A good narrative has a magnetic appeal; it draws the listener into the story. The listener becomes more of a participant than a spectator. A good narrative challenges the listener to think about who she is in light of the issues of the narrative. Narratives are very powerful elements in the human condition. They inform our actions through the formation of our conscience and character.

Narratives provide answers to such questions as: What does it means to be a person? What does it mean to flourish? Who "counts" in moral considerations? These fundamental questions are addressed even in the simplest narratives. The next time you watch television, for example, see how the show you watch responds to these questions. What does the show say (or imply) about human nature? Pay attention also to the commercials for the messages they give about the characteristics of being human or what it means to be fulfilled or happy. See who "counts" in these stories.

Narratives are not only fundamental; they are ubiquitous. They are everywhere! Given the fact that we are surrounded by narratives and that these many narratives clamor for our attention, people need interpretive tools. We all have a collection of narratives to help us navigate between the competing narratives and to process our experiences. Arguably the most powerful narratives in most peoples' lives are cultural narratives. A dominant narrative of our culture, one that does serve as the primary narrative for many, is that we ought to love ourselves especially through loving (in the sense of desiring or pursuing) material things. Our culture promotes the importance of having things.

This book has presented an alternative vision. It holds that first and foremost, we ought to love justice. This vision is supported by biblical narratives and reflection on fundamental human relationships. The imperative then is we ought to love (as in strongly desire) rightly ordered relationships in our lives. We ought to work to create the conditions in which persons, including ourselves, will flourish.

The notion that justice is the moral bond of relationships was repeated often in this text. This description of justice indicates an important distinction between justice and charity (defined as giving). Justice is not so much about giving things as it is about relationships. This point needs to be clarified. We saw in our discussion of distributive justice and common goods that material things are necessary for human flourishing. Justice ought to direct how such goods are produced and distributed. Justice is, however, about more than the equitable distribution of such goods. Justice requires fair distribution of goods because is sees such distribution as the foundation for appropriate relations between people. Justice is about internal relationships in families. It is about internal relationships in schools and businesses and organizations. It is about internal relationships in communities. It is about internal relationships in countries. It is about internal relationships within the human community. Justice is also about relations between these groups. Justice then is not so much about giving things, charity, government programs, etc., to people as it is about promoting right relationships between people. A moral relationship is one that respects the concrete reality of the other person. The just person is aware how his actions and attitudes (as well as the actions and attitudes of groups and organizations to which he belongs) directly or indirectly affect the well-being of others.

The Christian tradition is full, packed full, of narratives of people who have worked for justice. Indeed the strongest "argument" for Christianity is the lives of these people of faith dedicated to justice. In every generation, in the face of every injustice, Christians have taken stands and lived their lives as witnesses against injustice. Here is a representative list of such people: John Chrysostom, Patrick, Francis and Clare of Assisi, Bartolome de las Casas, Catherine of Siena, John Calvin, John Wesley, Sarah Grimke, Franz Jagerstatter, Dorothy Day, Martin Luther King Jr., Daniel Berrigan, Penny Lernoux, Oscar Romero, Rigoberta Menchu. The call today is that we become more aware of the Christian tradition of justice and that individual Christians come to be witnesses for justice in their lives.

Prophets and Justice

Narratives, cultural or otherwise, often do not afford the conditions for their own critique and transcendence. We are so much a part of the narratives, or perhaps better stated, they are so much a part of us, that we have a hard time standing outside of them. We often (and I am including myself in this) become stuck in a cultural trance, simply accepting dominant social narratives as the Truth. (Buy things. Be an individual. Buy more things. Success is measured by dollar signs. Buy a few more things. Look out for yourself. People in power always make the right choices.) We need prophets to shake us, to wake us from this trance. Prophets, though always controversial, are a necessary element of a community's moral health.

I have met a few prophets in my life. These meetings were not comfortable experiences. Prophets expect something of you. The last time I had a prophet speak in my class, he successfully undermined my whole teaching project. This particular prophet told my students that sitting and reading about justice within the protected walls of a college classroom was absurd. If we really wanted to learn about justice, we ought to be out in the streets experiencing poverty and oppression. That's where you learn about justice, he said. In a sense, of course, he was right but nonetheless his message was unsettling for me and my students.

Prophetic discourse, passionate in its plea, unrelenting in its critique, can alienate people as much as it can move people. Prophets spark resentment. Their "effectiveness," moreover, is not immediate. One could argue, for example, that Jesus was not very "effective" in his lifetime. People are more likely to be open to hearing the words of prophets after they have passed away!

Prophetic discourse is crucial to moral conversation and is indeed an integral part of moral development. Without prophets rising above cultural practices, what would our current policy be on human rights or on slavery or on the role of women or on the role of children in the workplace or on the number of deadly land mines scattered around the globe? Prophets played (and continue to play) significant roles in ending these violations of human dignity. Prophetic discourse is a necessary feature of moral communication, yet it needs to be pushed further.

Consider the example of sexual harassment policy in our schools and places of work. The stages in the development of policy can be described by the forms of moral discourse. Narrative: Women, victims of harassment, began to tell their stories. Prophetic: From the midst of these narratives, people arose to make the stories public. The impact was not only a condemnation of individual harassers, but an indictment of the structures within which this harassment occurred. Prophets pointed out that these were not isolated events. The patterns of this abuse illustrated issues concerning social attitudes toward women. Ethics: Critique was not enough to change structures. The victims, vulnerable by definition, were not themselves in positions of power to change the dominant patterns of social interaction. They had to translate their experience into the language that people who were not victims might understand. That is to say, they had to engage in ethical discourse. They had to give reasons for their positions. They had to make distinctions. They had to name and define what is meant by "harassment." They had to clearly and convincingly describe why certain types of behavior are morally unacceptable. These three stages necessarily lead to a fourth. Defining and describing the problem and arguing why it is an offense to human dignity will not stop it. There needs to be specific, direct, and effective policy to address the problem. Good policy and moral policy are not necessarily the same. Good policy cannot remove all instances of harassment everywhere, but within certain situations it can prohibit specific behavior. It can offer disincentives, termination of one's job, for example, in response to certain actions. People vulnerable to harassment ought to have concrete protection.

There is yet another stage. This movement from narrative to prophetic to ethical to policy must be done in such a way so as to engage the hearts and minds of communal members. It is hoped that over time the harassment policy, with its "negative" proscriptions outlawing certain types of behavior will ultimately lead to "positive" outcomes, namely, greater respect and justice for persons within the organization. The ultimate point is to change the cultural narrative. Harassment policy seeks to replace an attitude that tolerates or does not take abuse seriously with the idea that every person is entitled to basic respect. The initial harassers might not change their attitudes but maybe members of the next generation will change.

The call for today is that individual Christians and Christian communities have the strength to transcend the dominant cultural trance and become aware of the oppressive and abusive relationships both close to home and across the globe. Through the grace of God they are enabled to speak out against injustice and maintain the strength of conviction as they themselves are ignored or ridiculed. It is hard to imagine a moral society without prophets.

Ethics and Justice

Ethical discourse, in its search for clarity, in its search for reasonable positions, tends to be drier and less exciting work than narrative or prophetic discourse. Recall the example of harassment. Harassment is one of the things that one knows when one sees it, or better stated, one knows when one has been harassed. Defining it, describing it on paper is an altogether different matter. Ethics can be tedious. The wording must be painstakingly accurate. How would you, for example, define harassment in a way that is clear, comprehensive, and concise? If there is to be moral development, the narratives must be made "public" and the passionate pleas of the prophets ought to be translated into rationally defensible positions. The narratives must be presented in a meditating language, a language that those who are not victims can understand. Clear thinking, precise use of words, and compelling reasoning are essential components of moral communication. Ideas make a difference. This book included both narratives and definitions. You may have found the sections that included personal narratives more interesting than the sections that defined and described justice, but I remain hopeful that these sections were useful to you even in their dryness.

Justice is a comprehensive moral concept. Its significance extends into all areas of human relationships (and possibly to relations humans have to animals). Justice is a personal disposition, a character trait, that primarily reveals itself in the active responsibility one has towards others. As the traditional wording goes, justice means giving the other what is due. People are "due" things because of their individuality, because of the particular relationships they have to one another, and because of their relationship to all other persons based on common humanity.

The four forms of discourse evoke models for responsible leadership in justice. Some moral leaders, perhaps you know people like this, lead by example. They are "quiet" moral leaders. They do not do much talking, however their lives are models of justice. They are concerned with the content and direction of all the relationships they are in. Their concern for justice is often contagious to those who are close to them. These leaders are not likely to express themselves with the boldness of prophets. Maybe they are not in positions to decide policy. They are moral leaders nonetheless. Leaders for justice from within the ethical framework have a different vocation. They labor to convince others by reason. These are people who have hope in the power of reason and dialogue. They believe that a community can rationally come together for justice, and they know ethical language can expose the inconsistencies and hypocrisies of some public moral positions.

The call for today then is for articulate, clear thinking, persuasive people to take the cause of justice into public forums. My friend, the prophet, underestimates the importance of reasoned arguments. One way that the voices of the poor and vulnerable will be heard is through the mediating language of ethics. There are many among us who value appeals to the head as much as or more than appeals to the heart.

Policy and Justice

There are incidents of injustice and there are patterns of injustice. It is hard to legislate against the former, but it is necessary to legislate against the latter. If a pattern of injustice is not addressed by some level of formal policy within a community, such injustice is condoned by the community. Sexual harassment and racial discrimination are examples of this. As a community we took concrete steps to discourage and limit these activities. There remains much work to be done. A vulnerable class of people today in our society are children, especially children who grow up in poverty. Their well-being, their health, their education, the environment in which they grow up, ought to be a primary consideration of public policy.

The examples of harassment, racism, and the well-being of children illustrate the role that social justice plays in relation to the other areas of justice and indeed to policy concerns. As social justice looks at patterns of social interaction, it circumscribes interpersonal, commutative, distributive, and communal justice. Harassment, racism, and the well-being of children are not "private" matters. Although they occur in interpersonal or commutative realms, these injustices have significant social implications, and communities have an interest in protecting persons in these "private" matters. Social justice, in certain circumstances, can reach into and dictate characteristics of relationships within the other areas of justice. In employment, for example, if the dominant modes of operation have historically excluded members of certain groups, social justice claims can enforce policies to encourage the well-being of individual members of these groups. If sexual harassment occurs within the normal operations of an organization, social justice can override the culture of the group and regulate it. If children from families with lower incomes are receiving a less substantial education or limited access to basic health care than those from higher income families, social justice can make claims. Social justice, as it promotes the well-being of the vulnerable, ought to have a directive influence on public policy initiatives.

Let's review the five areas of justice, starting with social justice, and suggest how they might influence policy.

Social justice: Social justice shares a common starting point with policy discourse. Both begin with the question, "What is going on?" The criteria for discernment of what is going on are, however, different. Social justice, by definition, addresses this question from the perspective of the vulnerable. Policy may or may not do this. Social justice, by definition, focuses on larger patterns of interaction within and between communities. Policy may or may not do this. A policy that is informed by justice will, however, be informed by these criteria. On the other hand, social justice concerns are not necessarily limited by the question, "What is possible?" Persons working for social justice do not expect immediate results. "What is possible?" to them does not mean what is possible today or even what is possible in the immediate future. It might mean, however, what is possible in the long term. Persons working for social justice realize that structural change takes a long time. They are in it for the long haul. Policymakers must, however, address this limiting question. They need to be directed by the "What is possible for us to do in our particular context with our limited means?" question. To promote a law that is not feasible, though ethically rooted, is to promote a bad law.

Social justice advocates Joe Holland and Peter Henriot provide a model for understanding the "What is going on?" question or as they refer to it, social analysis. Social analysis is "the effort to obtain a more complete picture of a social situation by exploring its historical and structural relationships."[42] They state that this analysis looks at *issues*, such as unemployment, inflation, or hunger; *policies* that address these issues; *social structures*, such as education, law, business, patterns of production and distribution of goods, interest groups, unions, etc; and *societal divisions* such as race, sex, age, class, ethnicity, religion, and geography. Social analysis is both historical and structural. It examines the history and tradition of these issues, policies, structures, and divisions as well as how they appear in the present context.

Holland and Henriot give several examples of social analysis including the situation of migrant workers. They write, "The issue is not whether an individual grower in the Fresno Valley of California is a good or a malevolent person. Rather, the issue is the system of economic relationships between owner and producer and factors such as labor availability, land tenure, access to market, competition, etc., that lead to the exploitation of the unprotected migrant workers."[43] They offer three interesting questions to examine socioeconomic relationships: 1. Who makes the decisions? 2. Who benefits from the decisions? 3. Who bears the cost of such decisions?[44] The National Conference of Catholic Bishops offers a similar line of thinking in the first paragraph of its letter on the economy. The bishops write: "Every perspective on economic life that is human, moral, and Christian must be shaped by three questions: What does the economy do for people? What does it do to people? And how do people participate in it?"[45] Social justice and policy begin with an evaluation of the current reality. Social justice brings concern for the vulnerable to the table, a table usually occupied by the powerful.

Donal Dorr, in his book *The Social Justice Agenda*, lists over a dozen areas of social justice concerns today. He describes the population explosion and its link to poverty; the use of land in Third World countries where the production of coffee, tea, fruit, beef, and flowers for export are the priority and not enough food is produced for local people; the related question of the environment and wasteful use of resources; economic and political refugees; structural unemployment; the role of women; racism; human rights; the international debt; use of violence to obtain political ends; oppression among and within nations; disarmament and the sale of weapons to Third World countries; and the large gap between rich and poor, both across the globe, within countries, and within local communities.

His discussion of the final point (which he lists first) suggests some help in considering the relation between social justice and policy. Dorr argues, "The mere fact that some people are more wealthy than others is not, in itself, a social injustice. But the existence of gross poverty alongside conspicuous wealth is morally unacceptable. The fact that in our world millions of people do not have the basic necessities of life while others live in luxury is a basic injustice: it infringes the most fundamental human right of all—the right to life."[46] This situation of wealth disparity is complicated and is supported by international trade relations. Dorr continues, "If we are content to go along with the existing situation, without attempting to change the structures, then we are colluding in injustice. Many of us claim to know little or nothing about international economics or structures of injustice; but this convenient ignorance can hardly relieve us of all responsibility for the poverty and powerlessness of others which allows us to buy products at an unduly low price."[47] Social justice pushes us on responsibility. It demands that we examine the relationships we participate in and the character of the bonds of those relationships. Buying and selling merchandise establishes a bond between producers, distributors, marketers, sales people, and consumers. The ultimate say rests with the final step, namely, the consumer putting forth money to support the system. Social justice, broad in its scope, ultimately falls upon the actions of individuals.

Social justice is a process that includes gathering of facts, social analysis, and consideration of possibilities. An important tool in the contemporary pursuit of justice is the world-wide web. Information that was once private or hard to get can now be attained instantly. Resources for social analysis and justice concerns can easily be explored. There are many groups that keep the concern of the eighth century prophets alive and help us think through the contemporary social justice implications. Here are some examples of Christian organizations that provide helpful information: Sojourners, Catholic Worker, Pax Christi, Center of Concern, Evangelicals for Social Action, Salt of the Earth, NETWORK, Bread for the World, Campaign for Human Development, and The Interfaith Center on Corporate Responsibility. There are also many other resources, such as the U.S. Department of State, Amnesty International, and the Children's Defense Fund, that provide essential data.

Communal justice: Participation in local community, including one's neighborhood or church, is an essential part of promoting the greater common good. This participation should be encouraged but ought not be shortsighted. I think the "hourglass effect" presented in the Hebrew Scriptures is a helpful image here. We must focus on the immediate and local while always opening up to and being responsive to the broader communities in which we participate. This is not an either/or situation. We ought not play one off the other. This is a both/and situation. We must promote the social good of both our local communities and the wider communities. Social justice, always looking at the bigger picture, challenges us to consider how our local communities can work for justice within larger communities.

This is not to say that we must be involved in every movement or volunteer possibility that comes our way. My family and I must be on the mailing list of every group in society that survives on donations. At least four days a week we get some request from nonprofit groups, schools, church, church organizations, antipoverty groups, justice groups, peace groups, environmental groups, art organizations, museums, political parties, etc., requesting our support. If we were to support them all, we would be out on the street asking others to support us! We have to decide which organizations, which populations, which projects seem most important to us at this present time. Individuals, families, organizations have to examine truthfully their abilities and their resources to find avenues to promote the common good of the communities to which they belong.

Distributive justice: Distributive justice is the area of justice most related to policy issues. Government plays a crucial role here as it creates policy to direct the allocation of social goods and burdens. Policy ought to ensure that the vulnerable be provided fundamental human goods. This is not an optional role of the state. Government ought to see to it that public goods, communal goods, and procedural goods are fairly distributed throughout the community. Equitable distribution of these goods is a vital element of the common good.

Commutative justice: The dominant issue of commutative justice is the equitable distribution of income within businesses. In the American context, the disparity in compensation between labor and management is striking. The variety of compensation structures, wages and other forms, is based on distinctions within organizations that may not be rationally or ethically justified. Social justice especially challenges the exploitation of workers in very poor countries. Corporations based in richer countries often produce or buy products made under conditions of near slavery. There are shocking reports of poverty-level wages, dangerous working conditions, physical and other types of intimidation against workers, and forced production quotas associated with the production of toys in China, athletic shoes in Vietnam, soccer balls in Pakistan, and rugs in India. When we buy these products, we support the people who dictate these working conditions.

In the United States there are many different brands of toys, shoes, soccer balls, and rugs available for purchase. We are not forced to participate in such exploitation. Social justice concerns can pressure corporations to adjust their policies regarding treatment of workers. From a justice perspective, this is not an optional issue. When foreign governments oppress their citizens, there is often a response in the U.S. public arena. On the other hand, when we consumers support oppressive market structures, we do not want to acknowledge it. (Wearing certain brand-name clothing is too important for our image.) It is time to change this.

Interpersonal justice: The area of friendships, families, and intimate relationships seems quite foreign to policy issues. Certainly families can have "policies" for the distribution of their goods. As stated above, public policy, motivated by social justice concerns, ought to protect the well-being of the vulnerable. Social justice then can override the legitimate autonomy of a family when the demands of safety for children are in question, or it can limit the freedom of fathers (garnish their wages) who have abandoned their children.

As the directive form of justice, social justice demands a certain steadfastness and is closely allied with the prophetic form of moral discourse. Social justice advocates challenge structures of dominance through challenging the attitudes and "structures of the mind" of persons who participate, directly and indirectly, in these structures. The call for today then is for persons willing to make concrete policy proposals within their businesses, the organizations to which they belong, and the communities in which they live and participate so as to give others their due, especially their due based on common humanity.

All of this suggests that justice is not only a matter of the heart but of the mind as well. To love justice, to do justice, to be just requires that we see ourselves as *participants*, responsible participants, in a variety of relationships from the intimate to the impersonal. To love justice, to do justice, to be just requires, moreover, the willingness to *discern* what justice demands in these relationships.[48] The final words of this book have to go to the prophet Micah.

> "He has told you, O mortal, what is good;
> and what does the LORD require of you
> but to do justice, and to love kindness,
> and to walk humbly with your God" (6:8).

Notes

PREFACE

1. See James Gustafson, *Varieties of Moral Discourse: Prophetic, Narrative, Ethical, and Policy* (Grand Rapids: Calvin College and Seminary, 1988). Gustafson uses these distinctions in relation to environmental ethics in *A Sense of the Divine* (Cleveland: The Pilgrim Press, 1994) and in relation to medical ethics in "Moral Discourse about Medicine: A Variety of Forms," *The Journal of Medicine and Philosophy* 15 (1990): 125–42.

2. James Gustafson, *Ethics from a Theocentric Perspective: Theology and Ethics* (Chicago: University of Chicago Press, 1981), 69.

3. Gustafson, *Varieties of Moral Discourse*, 47.

4. Ibid.

5. James Gustafson, *Can Ethics Be Christian?* (Chicago: University of Chicago Press, 1975), 101.

CHAPTER ONE

1. See Robert Inchausti, *The Ignorant Perfection of Ordinary People* (Albany: SUNY, 1991), 51. Stanley Hauerwas believes, "There is no more fundamental way to talk of God than in a story." *The Peaceable Kingdom: A Primer in Christian Ethics* (Notre Dame: University of Notre Dame Press, 1983), 24.

2. Richard Gula, *Reason Informed by Faith* (New York: Paulist Press, 1989), 142.

3. Gustafson, *Varieties of Moral Discourse*, 22.

4. Ibid., 21.

5. William Spohn, "Parable and Narrative in Christian Ethics," *Theological Studies* 51 (1990): 102.

6. Michael Perry, *Love and Power: The Role of Religion and Morality in American Politics* (New York: Oxford University Press, 1991), 106.

7. Ibid.

8. Gula, *Reason Informed by Faith*, 166.

9. Raymond Brown and Sandra Schneiders, "Hermeneutics" in Raymond Brown, Joseph Fitzmeyer, Roland Murphy, eds., *The New Jerome Biblical Commentary* (Englewood Cliffs, New Jersey: Prentice Hall, 1990), 1156.

10. Gula, *Reason Informed by Faith*, 166.

11. James Gustafson, "The Place of Scripture in Christian Ethics: A Methological Study," in Charles Curran and Richard McCormick, eds., *Readings in Moral Theology No. 4: The Use of Scripture in Moral Theology* (New York: Paulist Press, 1984), 164–65.

12. William Spohn, *What Are They Saying about Scripture and Ethics?* (New York: Paulist Press, 1995), 6.

13. Richard Hays, *The Moral Vision of the New Testament: A Contemporary Introduction to New Testament Ethics* (San Francisco: Harper Collins, 1996), 310.

14. Brown and Schneiders, "Hermeneutics," 1147.

15. Ibid.

16. Ibid., 1147–48.

17. National Conference of Catholic Bishops, *The Challenge of Peace: God's Promise and Our Response* in David O'Brien and Thomas Shannon, eds., *Catholic Social Thought: The Documentary Heritage* (Maryknoll, N.Y.: Orbis Books, 1992), #28.

18. Lisa Sowle Cahill, *Between the Sexes: Foundations for a Christian Ethics of Sexuality* (New York: Paulist Press, 1985), 62.

19. Hays, *The Moral Vision of the New Testament*, 299. Stanley Hauerwas argues that such selectivity is arbitrary. See "The Moral Authority of Scripture: The Politics and Ethics of Remembering" in Curran and McCormick, eds., *Readings in Moral Theology No. 4*.

20. Gula, *Reason Informed by Faith*, 165.

21. Lisa Sowle Cahill, *Women and Sexuality* (New York: Paulist Press, 1993), 42–43.

22. Gula, *Reason Informed by Faith*, 168.

23. Hauerwas, "The Moral Authority of Scripture," 253

24. Brown and Schneiders, "Hermeneutics," 1153.

25. Spohn, *What Are They Saying about Scripture and Ethics?*, 95.

26. Ibid., 94.

27. Pauline Viviano, *Genesis* (Collegeville, Minn.: The Liturgical Press, 1985), 13.

28. James Nash, *Loving Nature: Ecological Integrity and Christian Responsibility* (Nashville: Abingdon Press, 1991), 96.

29. Ibid., 104.

30. See Ibid.; Viviano, *Genesis*, 13; Robert Davidson, *Genesis 1–11* (Cambridge: Cambridge University Press, 1973), 25; Richard Clifford and Roland

Murphy, "Genesis," in Brown, Fitzmeyer, and Murphy, eds., *The New Jerome Biblical Commentary*, 9; John Gidson, *Genesis* (Philadelphia: Westminster Press, 1981), 67.

31. Jon Levenson, *Creation and the Persistence of Evil* (Princeton: Princeton University Press, 1988), 116.

32. Nash, *Loving Nature*, 106.

33. National Conference of Catholic Bishops, *Economic Justice for All: Pastoral Letter on Catholic Social Teaching and the U.S. Economy* in O'Brien and Shannon, eds., *Catholic Social Thought*, #32.

34. Claus Westermann, *Genesis: An Introduction* (Minneapolis: Fortress Press, 1992), 111.

35. This distinction is James Gustafson's. See "The Place of Scripture in Christian Ethics," and Gula, *Reason Informed by Faith*, 168.

36. Levenson, *Creation and the Persistence of Evil*, 127.

37. Nash, *Loving Nature*, 104.

38. Clifford and Murphy, "Genesis" in Brown, Fitzmeyer, and Murphy, eds., *The New Jerome Biblical Commentary*, 8.

39. Bruce Birch, *Let Justice Roll Down: The Old Testament, Ethics and Christian Life* (Louisville: Westminster/John Knox, 1991), 115.

40. Bruce Metzger and Roland Murphy, eds., *The New Oxford Annotated Bible* (New York: Oxford University Press, 1991), 69.

41. Birch, *Let Justice Roll Down*, 114–15.

42. Gustavo Gutierrez, *A Theology of Liberation* (Maryknoll, N.Y.: Orbis Books, 1988), 90.

43. Metzger and Murphy, eds., *The New Oxford Annotated Bible*, xxxv.

44. Birch, *Let Justice Roll Down*, 131.

45. See Karen Lebacqz, *Justice in an Unjust World: Foundations for a Christian Approach to Justice* (Minneapolis: Augsburg Publishing House, 1987).

46. My colleague Corrine Patton directed me on this point.

47. Martin Luther King Jr., *Stength to Love* (Philadelphia: Fortress Press, 1983), 81.

CHAPTER TWO

1. The Book of Isaiah has sixty-six chapters. It was written in three time periods by three authors. Most of the first section, chapters 1–39, was written by Isaiah himself in the eighth century. See for example the articles "Isaiah" and "Deutero-Isaiah and Trito-Isaiah" in Brown, Fitzmeyer, and Murphy, eds., *The New Jerome Biblical Commentary*.

2. Gerhard von Rad, *The Message of the Prophets* (New York: Harper and Row, 1965), 100.

3. Thomas Wahl, Irene Nowell, and Anthony Ceresko, "Zephaniah, Nahum, Habakkuk" in Brown, Fitzmeyer, and Murphy, eds., *The New Jerome Biblical Commentary*, 255. See also von Rad, *The Message of the Prophets*, 100.

4. Joseph Jensen and William Irwin, "Isaiah 1–39" in Brown, Fitzmeyer, and Murphy, eds., *The New Jerome Biblical Commentary*, 230.

5. John Miller, *Meet the Prophets: A Beginner's Guide to the Books of the Biblical Prophets* (New York: Paulist Press, 1987), 82.

6. Thomas Ogletree, *The Use of the Bible in Christian Ethics* (Philadelphia: Fortress Press, 1983), 66.

7. Brich, *Let Justice Roll Down*, 256.

8. Michael Barre, "Amos" in Brown, Fitzmeyer, and Murphy, eds., *The New Jerome Biblical Commentary*, 212.

9. Ibid., 213.

10. See William Doorly, *Prophet of Justice: Understanding the Book of Amos* (New York: Paulist Press, 1989), 73–76.

11. Dennis McCarthy and Roland Murphy, "Hosea" in Brown, Fitzmeyer, and Murphy, eds., *The New Jerome Biblical Commentary*, 226.

12. Moshe Weinfeld, *Social Justice in Ancient Israel and in the Ancient Near East* (Minneapolis: Fortress Press, 1995), 37.

13. John Barton, "Ethics in Isaiah of Jerusalem" in Robert Gordon, ed., *The Place Is Too Small for Us: Israelite Prophets in Recent Scholarship* (Winona Lake, Ind.: Eisenbrauns, 1995), 86.

14. Thomas Aquinas, *Summa Theologica* (New York: Benzinger Brothers, 1947), I-II, Q. 96, Art. 5.

15. Martin Luther King Jr., "Letter from a Birmingham Jail" in James Washington, ed., *I Have a Dream: Writing and Speeches That Changed the World* (San Francisco: Harper Collins, 1992), 89.

16. Weinfeld, *Social Justice in Ancient Israel and in the Ancient Near East*, 44.

17. Karl Marx, "Communist Manifesto" in Robert Tucker, ed., *The Marx-Engels Reader* (New York: W.W. Norton, 1972), 362.

18. Donal Dorr, *Option for the Poor: A Hundred Years of Catholic Social Thought* (Maryknoll, N.Y.: Orbis Books, 1992), 253.

19. Ogletree, *The Use of the Bible in Christian Ethics*, 68.

20. Inchausti, *The Ignorant Perfection of Ordinary People,* 116.

21. Walter Brueggemann, *The Prophetic Imagination* (Minneapolis: Fortress Press, 1978), 13.

22. Other characteristics of Hebrew prophets that are not necessary elements of contemporary prophets or prophetic discourse are ecstatic experiences and miracle working.

23. Jim Wallis, *The Soul of Politics: A Practical and Prophetic Vision for Change* (New York: The New Press, 1994), 45.

24. Jon Sobrino, *Archbishop Romero: Memories and Reflections* (Maryknoll, N.Y.: Orbis Books, 1990), 103.

25. Gutierrez, *A Theology of Liberation*, 152.

26. King, *I Have a Dream*, 97.

27. Dorothy Day, *The Long Loneliness* (San Francisco: HarperCollins, 1981), 150.

28. Bruce Vawter, "Introduction to Prophetic Literature," in Brown, Fitzmeyer, Murphy, eds., *The New Jerome Biblical Commentary*, 196.

29. Gustafson, *Varieties of Moral Discourse*, 8.

30. Cornel West, *Race Matters* (New York, Vintage Books, 1994), 19.

31. Ibid., 20.

32. Dorr, *Option for the Poor*, 253.

33. John Paul II, *Sollicitudo Rei Socialis* in O'Brien and Shannon, eds., *Catholic Social Thought*, 65.

34. Wallis, *The Soul of Politics*, 152.

35. See text in King, *I Have a Dream.*

36. Sobrino, *Archbishop Romero*, 149.

37. Gutierrez, *A Theology of Liberation*, 152.

38. Sobrino, *Archbishop Romero*, 104.

39. Gutierrez, *A Theology of Liberation*, 136.

40. Gustafson, *Varieties of Moral Discourse*, 13.

41. King, *I Have a Dream*, 104.

42. Gustafson, *Varieties of Moral Discourse*, 14.

43. Gutierrez, *A Theology of Liberation*, 233.

44. Sobrino, *Archbishop Romero*, 109.

45. Wallis, *The Soul of Politics*, 236.

46. Vawter, "Introduction to Prophetic Literature," 189.

47. *Didache*, in Cyril Richardson, ed., *Early Christian Fathers* (New York: Collier Books, 1970), 177.

48. Ibid.

49. Vawter, "Introduction to Prophetic Literature," 189.

50. Ibid., 194.

51. Gustafson, *Varieties of Moral Discourse*, 9.

52. King, *I Have a Dream*, 91.

53. Day, *The Long Loneliness*, 222.

54. Ellsberg, *Dorothy Day: Selected Writings*, xxx.

55. Gustafson, *Varieties of Moral Discourse*, 16–17.

CHAPTER THREE

1. Weinfeld, *Social Justice in Ancient Israel and in the Ancient Near East*, 20.

2. Ibid.

3. Michael Himes and Kenneth Himes, *Fullness of Faith: The Public Significance of Theology* (New York: Paulist Press, 1993), 135.

4. Spohn, *What Are They Saying about Scripture and Ethics?*, 101.

5. Gutierrez, *A Theology of Liberation*, xxvi.

6. Miller, *Meet the Prophets*, 53.

7. Levenson, *Creation and the Persistence of Evil*, 104.

8. King, *Strength to Love,* 30.

9. Jerome Kodell, *The Gospel According to Luke* (Collegeville, Minn.: The Liturgical Press, 1983), 61.

10. Shusaku Endo, *Deep River* (New York: New Directions Books, 1994), 103.

11. Inchausti, *The Ignorant Perfection of Ordinary People*, 74.

12. Robert Karris, "The Gospel According to Luke" in Brown, Fitzmeyer, and Murphy, eds., *The New Jerome Biblical Commentary*, 703.

13. Allen Verhey, *The Great Reversal: Ethics and the New Testament* (Grand Rapids, Mich.: William Eerdmans Publishing Co., 1984), 19.

14. Metzger and Murphy, eds. *The New Oxford Annotated Bible,* NT 98.

15. Verhey, *The Great Reversal*, 11.

16. Edward Schillebeeckx, *Jesus: An Experiment in Christology* (New York: Crossroad, 1981), 142.

17. William Johnson Evertt, *God's Federal Republic: Reconstructing Our Governing Symbol* (New York: Paulist Press, 1988), 52–53, argues "The problem with kingship lies in the way it obstructs the development of a truly public realm in which people are bound together in arguments, promises, reason, and convictions about their common life and the world they inhabit. It seeks the order of the household rather than the clamor of the fair, the silence of the Father's final word rather than the many words of citizens in argument, the inequality that makes possible coercion rather than the equality that demands respectful reasoning."

18. Gula, *Reason Informed by Faith*, 174

19. Gutierrez, *A Theology of Liberation*, 135.

20. Jose Miranda, *Communism in the Bible* (Maryknoll, N.Y.: Orbis Books, 1985), argues that the kingdom is on earth. See especially pages 12–17.

21. National Conference of Catholic Bishops, *The Challenge of Peace* in O'Brien and Shannon, eds., *Catholic Social Thought*, #58.

22. Benedict Viviano, "Matthew," in Brown, Fitzmeyer, and Murphy, eds., *The New Jerome Biblical Commentary*, 639.

23. See Verhey, *The Great Reversal*, 21.

24. See Gula, *Reason Informed by Faith*, 174–179.

25. Verhey, *The Great Reversal*, 15.

26. Ibid.

27. Quoted in Day, *The Long Loneliness*, 280.

CHAPTER FOUR

1. Day, *The Long Loneliness*, 244.

2. Stanley Hauerwas, *A Community of Character* (Notre Dame: University of Notre Dame Press, 1981), 109.

3. Hays, *The Moral Vision of the New Testament*, 469.

4. Ibid., 322.

5. Ibid., 196.

6. Ibid., 128.

7. Ibid., 135.

8. Synod of Bishops, *Justice in the World* in O'Brien and Shannon, eds., *Catholic Social Thought*, 289.

9. Paul VI, *Evangelii Nuntiandi*, in O'Brien and Shannon, eds., *Catholic Social Thought*, #30.

10. John Paul II, *Sollicitudo Rei Socialis* in O'Brien and Shannon, eds., *Catholic Social Thought*, #113.

11. Hays, *The Moral Vision of the New Testament*, 343.

12. Gustafson, *Can Ethics Be Christian?*, 163.

13. *The New Encyclopedia Britannica*, 15th ed., s.v. "Ethics."

14. Martha Nussbaum, "Human Functioning and Social Justice: In Defense of Aristotelian Essentialism," *Political Theory* 20, no. 2 (May 1992).

15. Ibid., 222–223.

16. Sylvia Ann Hewlett, *When the Bough Breaks: The Cost of Neglecting Our Children* (New York: HarperPerennial, 1991), 212–13.

17. See Spohn, "Parable and Narrative in Christian Ethics."

18. Lebacqz, *Justice in an Unjust World*, p.7.

19. What is referred to here as "ethical discourse" has been described in other places as moral philosophy and ethical theory. In theological contexts it has been referred to as moral theology or theological ethics. Not all commentators share this description discussed here.

20. See Philip Keane, *Health Care Reform: A Catholic View* (New York: Paulist Press, 1993) for an example of this.

21. Gustafson, *Varieties of Moral Discourse*, 42.

22. A number of sources were used for this section including Tom Beauchamp and James Childress, *Principles of Biomedical Ethics* (New York: Oxford University Press, 1994); William Frankena, *Ethics* (Englewood Cliffs, N.J.: Prentice Hall, 1973), and "Ethics" in *The New Encyclopedia Britannica*.

23. Frankena, *Ethics*, 34.

24. For contemporary discussion, see Michael Bayles, ed., *Contemporary Utilitarianism* (Garden City, N.Y.: Doubleday, 1968).

25. Immanuel Kant, *Groundwork for the Metaphysics of Morals* (Indianapolis: Bobbs-Merrill, 1979), 8–9.

26. Ibid., 39.

27. Ibid., 47.

28. Alan Donagan, *The Theory of Morality* (Chicago: University of Chicago Press, 1977) and John Rawls, *A Theory of Justice* (Cambridge, Mass.: Harvard University Press, 1971).

29. Ronald Dworkin, *Taking Rights Seriously* (Cambridge, Mass.: Harvard University Press, 1978), 172.

30. Ibid., xi.

31. United Nations General Assembly, "Universal Declaration of Human Rights," in Joseph Fahey and Richard Armstrong, eds., *A Peace Reader: Essential Readings on War, Justice, Non-Violence, and World Order* (New York: Paulist Press, 1992), 335.

32. See Alan Gewirth, *Human Rights: Essays on Justification and Applications* (Chicago: University of Chicago Press, 1982) and *Reason and Morality* (Chicago: University of Chicago Press, 1978).

33. Frankena, *Ethics*, 63.

34. Jean Porter, *The Recovery of Virtue: The Relevance of Aquinas for Christian Ethics* (Louisville: Westminster/John Knox, 1990), 70.

35. Beauchamp and Childress, *Principles of Biomedical Ethics*, 65.

36. Contemporary virtue theorists include Alasdair MacIntyre, *After Virtue* (Notre Dame: University of Notre Dame Press, 1984); and Philippa Foot, *Virtues and Vices* (Oxford: Basil Blackwell, 1978). See also Paul Wadell, *The Primacy of Love* (New York: Paulist Press, 1992).

37. Charles Taylor notes in his *Sources of the Self: The Making of the Modern Identity* (Cambridge, Mass.: Harvard University Press, 1989), 77: "This drive toward unification, far from being an essential feature of morality, is rather a peculiar feature of modern moral philosophy."

38. See Gutierrez, *A Theology of Liberation*.

39. Carol Gilligan, *In a Different Voice* (Cambridge, Mass.: Harvard University Press, 1982), 160.

40. Nel Noddings, *The Challenge to Care in Schools: An Alternative Approach to Education* (New York: Teachers College Press, 1992), 21.

41. Ibid.

42. Ibid., 24.

43. The phrase is from Susan Moller Okin, *Justice, Gender, and the Family* (San Franciso: Basic Books, 1989), 11. Okin argues here that all the prominent theories of justice, including some of the ethical theories mentioned here, have neglected the role of the family. See also Joan Tronto, *Moral Boundaries: A Political Argument for an Ethics of Care* (New York: Routledge, 1993).

44. The term is used by Herman Daly and John Cobb in *For the Common Good: Redirecting the Economy Toward Community, the Environment, and a Sustainable Future* (Boston: Beacon Press, 1989).

45. MacIntrye, *After Virtue*, 64–67.

46. For examples of communitarianism see for example, Robert Bellah, Richard Madsen, William Sullivan, Ann Swidler, and Steven Tipton, *Habits of the Heart: Individualism and Commitment in American Life* (San Francisco: Harper & Row, 1985); Amitai Etzioni, *The Spirit of Community: Rights, Responsibilities, and the Communitarian Agenda* (New York: Crown Books, 1993); and Philip Selznick, *The Moral Commonwealth: Social Theory and the Promise of Community* (Berkeley: University of California Press, 1992).

47. See James Gustafson, *Protestant and Roman Catholic Ethics: Prospects for Rapprochement* (Chicago: University of Chicago Press, 1978).

48. Taylor, *Sources of the Self*, 77.

49. Ibid., 89.

50. This phrase is taken from the National Conference of Catholic Bishops, *Economic Justice for All* in O'Brien and Shannon, eds., *Catholic Social Thought*, #79.

51. Selznick, *The Moral Commonwealth*, 434.

52. Aristotle, *Nicomachean Ethics* (Indianapolis: Bobbs-Merrill, 1983), 114 (book five, chapter one, 1129a). Aquinas quotes Aristotle here as he answers the question in *Summa Theologica*, II-II, Q. 58, Art. 12, "Whether Justice Stands Foremost Among All the Moral Virtues?"

CHAPTER FIVE

1. Ben Scripps, *Disney's the Hunchback of Notre Dame*, (Disney, 1996), http://www.uni-frankfurt.de/~fp/Disney/Scripts/HunchbackOfNotreDame.txt.

2. National Conference of Catholic Bishops, *Economic Justice for All*, in O'Brien and Shannon, eds., *Catholic Social Thought*, #71.

3. This is, of course, not the only place one could begin a reflection on morality and justice. The common experience of hunger, for example, would be another helpful starting point.

4. Hays, *The Moral Vision of the New Testament*, 154.

5. Wadell, *The Primacy of Love*, 65.

6. Ibid., 70.

7. Aristotle, *Nichomachean Ethics*, 215.

8. Ibid.

9. The idea that justice is a bond for a community is from Arthur Dyck, *Rights and Responsibilities: The Moral Bonds of Community* (Cleveland: The Pilgrim Press, 1994).

10. Margaret Farley, *Personal Commitments: Beginning, Keeping, Changing* (San Francisco: Harper & Row, 1986), 80.

11. Ibid.

12. Ibid., 81.

13. Ibid.

14. Judith Wallerstein supports this conclusion in her studies of divorce and happy marriages. In good marriages each partner has a high level of respect for the other. See Wallerstein, *The Good Marriage: How and Why Love Lasts* (Boston: Houghton Mifflin Company, 1995), 329.

15. Okin, *Justice, Gender, and the Family*, 9.

16. Wadell, *The Primacy of Love*, 71–72.

17. John Paul II, *On the Family* (Washington: United States Catholic Conference, 1981), 40.

18. Okin, *Justice, Gender, and the Family*, 17.

19. Ibid., 135.

20. David Hollenbach, *Justice, Peace and Human Rights: American Catholic Social Ethics in a Pluralistic Context* (New York: Crossroad, 1988), 20.

21. Okin, *Justice, Gender, and the Family*, 10. Continuing her commentary on contemporary theories of justice, Okin is right on target as she calls these writers to task because they never consider the institution of the family in light of the standards of justice they arrive at for society.

22. Albert Jonsen, "Responsibility" in James Childress and John Macquarrie, eds., *The Westminster Dictionary of Christian Ethics* (Philadelphia: Westminster Press, 1986).

23. Dworkin, *Taking Rights Seriously*, xi.

24. Gewirth, *Reason and Morality*, 65.

25. Ibid.

26. United Nations, "Universal Declaration of Human Rights" in Fahey and Armstrong, eds., *A Peace Reader*, 334.

27. Ibid., 335.

28. Jacques Maritain, *Man and the State* (Chicago: University of Chicago Press, 1951), 76.

29. Ibid., 77.

30. The most famous contemporary philosophical tirade against human rights language is found in MacIntyre's *After Virtue*, 67. MacIntyre writes, "the truth is plain: There are no such rights, and belief in them is one with belief in witches and in unicorns."

31. Henry Shue, *Basic Rights: Subsistence, Affluence, and U.S. Foreign Policy* (Princeton, N.J.: Princeton University Press, 1980), ix.

32. John XXIII, *Pacem in terris* in O'Brien and Shannon, eds., *Catholic Social Thought*, #11.

33. Michael Westmoreland-White, "Setting the Record Straight: Christian Faith, Human Rights, and the Enlightenment," in *The Annual of the Society of Christian Ethics* (1995): 95.

34. See for example, Aristotle, *Nichomachean Ethics*, 117.

35. David Hollenbach, *Claims in Conflict: Retrieving and Renewing the Catholic Human Rights Tradition* (New York: Paulist Press, 1979), 145.

36. Ibid.

37. Jon Gunnemann, "Capitalism and Commutative Justice" in Max Stackhouse, Dennis McCann, Shirley Roels, eds., *On Moral Business: Classical and Contemporary Resources for Ethics in Economic Life* (Grand Rapids, Mich.: William Eerdmans Publishing Co., 1995), 627.

38. National Conference of Catholic Bishops, *Economic Justice for All*, in O'Brien and Shannon, eds., *Catholic Social Thought*, #69.

39. Robert Bellah, Richard Madsen, William Sullivan, Ann Swidler, and Steven Tipton, *The Good Society* (New York: Alfred A. Knopf, 1991), 40.

40. Quoted in Bellah, *The Good Society*, 13.

41. John Paul II, *Sollicitudo Rei Socialis*, in O'Brien and Shannon, eds., *Catholic Social Thought*, # 65.

42. Michael Walzer, *Spheres of Justice: A Defense of Pluralism and Equality* (New York: Basic Books, 1983), 3–10, argues this point. I think, however, in our historical context, a case can be made for particular sets of such goods.

43. Douglas Sturm, "Toward a New Social Covenant: From Commodity to Commonwealth," in Bruce Grelle and David Krueger, eds., *Christianity and Capitalism* (Chicago: Center for the Scientific Study of Religion, 1986), 97.

44. Helen Prejean, *Dead Man Walking: An Eyewitness Account of the Death Penalty in the United States* (New York: Vintage Books, 1994), 50.

45. Gene Outka, "Social Justice and Equal Access to Health Care," in Stephen Lammers and Allen Verhey, eds., *On Moral Medicine: Theological Perspectives in Medical Ethics* (Grand Rapids, Mich.: William Eerdmans Publishing Co., 1987).

46. For a comprehensive commentary on Ryan, see Harlan Beckley, *Passion for Justice* (Louiseville: Westminster/John Knox Press, 1992).

47. Etzioni, *The Spirit of Community*, 263.

48. Ibid., 264.

49. Amy Guttman, *Multiculturalism* (Princeton: Princeton University Press, 1994), 22.

50. Selznick, *The Moral Commonwealth*, 370.

51. Laurent Parks Daloz, Cheryl Keen, James Keen, Sharon Daloz Parks, *Common Fire: Lives of Commitment in a Complex World* (Boston: Beacon Press, 1996), 64–65.

52. Tronto, *Moral Boundaries*, 35.

53. See Charles Curran in *Origins of Moral Theology in the United States* (Washington: Georgetown University Press, 1997).

54. Inchausti, *The Ignorant Perfection of Ordinary People*, 127.

55. Quoted in Inchausti, 126.

CHAPTER SIX

1. Wadell, *The Primacy of Love*, 132.

2. Ibid., 133.

3. John Langan, "Prudence," in Childress and Macquarrie, eds., *The Westminster Dictionary of Christian Ethics*, 515.

4. Andrew Campbell and Laura Nash, *A Sense of Mission: Defining Direction for the Large Corporation* (Reading, Mass.: Addison-Wesley Publishing Company, 1992), 10.

5. Ibid., 23.

6. See Gustafson, *A Sense of the Divine*, 129.

7. Ibid., 122.

8. Ibid., 125.

9. National Conference of Catholic Bishops, *Economic Justice for All,* in O'Brien and Shannon, eds., *Catholic Social Thought*, #134.

10. Gula, *Reason Informed by Faith*, 252.

11. Ibid., 253–54.

12. Stephen Carter, *The Culture of Disbelief: How American Law and Politics Trivialize Religious Devotion* (New York: Basic Books, 1993), 112.

13. Ibid., 106.

14. Ibid., 109.

15. Keane, *Health Care Reform*, 154.

16. See H. Richard Niebuhr, *Christ and Culture* (New York: Harper Collins, 1975).

17. Robin Lovin, *Religion and American Public Life: Interpretations and Explorations* (New York: Paulist Press, 1986), 15.

18. Perry, *Love and Power*, 77.

19. Himes and Himes, *Fullness of Faith*, 75.

20. Ibid., 79.

21. Ibid., 81.

22. Ibid., 96.

23. Lovin, *Religion and American Public Life* (New York: Paulist Press, 1986), 9.

24. Ibid., 16.

25. Warren Copeland, *And The Poor Get Welfare: The Ethics of Poverty in the United States* (Nashville: Abingdon Press, 1994), 89.

26. Keane, *Health Care Reform*, 156.

27. Himes and Himes, *Fullness of Faith*, 96.

28. Quoted in Perry, *Love and Power*, 107.

29. Lovin, *Religion and American Public Life*, 25–26.

30. Perry, *Love and Power*, 105.

31. Ibid., 106.

32. Ibid., 106.

33. Ibid., 107.

34. Ibid., 126.

35. Himes and Himes, *Fullness of Faith*, 96.

36. Ibid.

37. Keane, *Health Care Reform*, 166.

38. King, *I Have a Dream*, 25.

39. King, *A Testament of Hope*, 292–93.

40. Ibid., 124.

41. Aquinas, *Summa Theologica*, I-II, Q. 96, Art. 2, rel obj 2.

42. Joe Holland and Peter Henroit, *Social Analysis: Linking Faith and Justice* (Maryknoll, N.Y.: Orbis Books, 1985), 14.

43. Ibid., 24.

44. Ibid., 28.

45. National Conference of Catholic Bishops, *Economic Justice for All*, in O'Brien and Shannon, eds., *Catholic Social Thought*, #1.

46. Donal Dorr, *The Social Justice Agenda: Justice, Ecology, Power and the Church* (Maryknoll, N.Y.: Orbis Books, 1991), 8.

47. Ibid., 10.

48. James Gustafson highlights participation and discernment as crucial elements of the moral life. See *Ethics from a Theocentric Perspective, Volume One, Theology and Ethics,* especially chapter seven, and *Ethics from a Theocentric Perspective, Volume Two: Ethics and Theology,* especially chapter nine (Chicago: University of Chicago Press, 1984).

Index